Eighteenth Century
Collections Online
Print Editions

D1809884

Gale ECCO Print Editions

Relive history with *Eighteenth Century Collections Online*, now available in print for the independent historian and collector. This series includes the most significant English-language and foreign-language works printed in Great Britain during the eighteenth century, and is organized in seven different subject areas including literature and language; medicine, science, and technology; and religion and philosophy. The collection also includes thousands of important works from the Americas.

The eighteenth century has been called "The Age of Enlightenment." It was a period of rapid advance in print culture and publishing, in world exploration, and in the rapid growth of science and technology – all of which had a profound impact on the political and cultural landscape. At the end of the century the American Revolution, French Revolution and Industrial Revolution, perhaps three of the most significant events in modern history, set in motion developments that eventually dominated world political, economic, and social life.

In a groundbreaking effort, Gale initiated a revolution of its own: digitization of epic proportions to preserve these invaluable works in the largest online archive of its kind. Contributions from major world libraries constitute over 175,000 original printed works. Scanned images of the actual pages, rather than transcriptions, recreate the works *as they first appeared.*

Now for the first time, these high-quality digital scans of original works are available via print-on-demand, making them readily accessible to libraries, students, independent scholars, and readers of all ages.

For our initial release we have created seven robust collections to form one the world's most comprehensive catalogs of 18th century works.

Initial Gale ECCO Print Editions collections include:

History and Geography
Rich in titles on English life and social history, this collection spans the world as it was known to eighteenth-century historians and explorers. Titles include a wealth of travel accounts and diaries, histories of nations from throughout the world, and maps and charts of a world that was still being discovered. Students of the War of American Independence will find fascinating accounts from the British side of conflict.

Social Science

Delve into what it was like to live during the eighteenth century by reading the first-hand accounts of everyday people, including city dwellers and farmers, businessmen and bankers, artisans and merchants, artists and their patrons, politicians and their constituents. Original texts make the American, French, and Industrial revolutions vividly contemporary.

Medicine, Science and Technology

Medical theory and practice of the 1700s developed rapidly, as is evidenced by the extensive collection, which includes descriptions of diseases, their conditions, and treatments. Books on science and technology, agriculture, military technology, natural philosophy, even cookbooks, are all contained here.

Literature and Language

Western literary study flows out of eighteenth-century works by Alexander Pope, Daniel Defoe, Henry Fielding, Frances Burney, Denis Diderot, Johann Gottfried Herder, Johann Wolfgang von Goethe, and others. Experience the birth of the modern novel, or compare the development of language using dictionaries and grammar discourses.

Religion and Philosophy

The Age of Enlightenment profoundly enriched religious and philosophical understanding and continues to influence present-day thinking. Works collected here include masterpieces by David Hume, Immanuel Kant, and Jean-Jacques Rousseau, as well as religious sermons and moral debates on the issues of the day, such as the slave trade. The Age of Reason saw conflict between Protestantism and Catholicism transformed into one between faith and logic -- a debate that continues in the twenty-first century.

Law and Reference

This collection reveals the history of English common law and Empire law in a vastly changing world of British expansion. Dominating the legal field is the *Commentaries of the Law of England* by Sir William Blackstone, which first appeared in 1765. Reference works such as almanacs and catalogues continue to educate us by revealing the day-to-day workings of society.

Fine Arts

The eighteenth-century fascination with Greek and Roman antiquity followed the systematic excavation of the ruins at Pompeii and Herculaneum in southern Italy; and after 1750 a neoclassical style dominated all artistic fields. The titles here trace developments in mostly English-language works on painting, sculpture, architecture, music, theater, and other disciplines. Instructional works on musical instruments, catalogs of art objects, comic operas, and more are also included.

The BiblioLife Network

This project was made possible in part by the BiblioLife Network (BLN), a project aimed at addressing some of the huge challenges facing book preservationists around the world. The BLN includes libraries, library networks, archives, subject matter experts, online communities and library service providers. We believe every book ever published should be available as a high-quality print reproduction; printed on-demand anywhere in the world. This insures the ongoing accessibility of the content and helps generate sustainable revenue for the libraries and organizations that work to preserve these important materials.

The following book is in the "public domain" and represents an authentic reproduction of the text as printed by the original publisher. While we have attempted to accurately maintain the integrity of the original work, there are sometimes problems with the original work or the micro-film from which the books were digitized. This can result in minor errors in reproduction. Possible imperfections include missing and blurred pages, poor pictures, markings and other reproduction issues beyond our control. Because this work is culturally important, we have made it available as part of our commitment to protecting, preserving, and promoting the world's literature.

GUIDE TO FOLD-OUTS MAPS and OVERSIZED IMAGES

The book you are reading was digitized from microfilm captured over the past thirty to forty years. Years after the creation of the original microfilm, the book was converted to digital files and made available in an online database.

In an online database, page images do not need to conform to the size restrictions found in a printed book. When converting these images back into a printed bound book, the page sizes are standardized in ways that maintain the detail of the original. For large images, such as fold-out maps, the original page image is split into two or more pages

Guidelines used to determine how to split the page image follows:

• Some images are split vertically; large images require vertical and horizontal splits.
• For horizontal splits, the content is split left to right.
• For vertical splits, the content is split from top to bottom.
• For both vertical and horizontal splits, the image is processed from top left to bottom right.

IMPIETY
AND
SUPERSTITION
Expos'd:

A *Poetical* ESSAY.

With a Difcourfe by way of Preface, wherein is dif-
covered the Original of *Deifm, Libertinifm* and *Superftition,* the Three great Enemies of Religion.
And of the prefent Ceremonies of the Church of
Rome; draw'n partly from the old abolifh'd *Jewifh*
Oœconomy, and partly from the Pagan Rites, in-
vented by *Numa Pompilius,* &c.

By W. B. Gent.

Dum nihil habemus majus, Calamo ludimus,
Phædrus.

EDINBURGH,
Printed by *John Moncur,* and Sold by *John Vallange*
Book-Seller, at his Shop oppofite to the Entry to
the *Parliament*-Clofs. 1710.

ERRATA.

PAge 3 l. 4. for *hm*, read *him*. *Ibid. l* 5. *Reverence* r. *Rev'rence.* p 13. l. 20. for r. *fo.* p 14 l 8 for e for *thie* l. 15. *fire* r *hue.* Ibid. l. 17. *down* r *doom.* p. 15 l. 5. *Malloch* r. *Moloch.* p 36. l 9. *scarscely* r. *scarcely.* p. 56. l. 23. *bring* r. *bring.* p. 62 l. 4. *pablick* r *pablick.* Ibid. l. 9. *Daphness* r. *Daphne's.*

To the Right Honourable,

Sir PATRICK JOHNSTON
Lord Provoft;

ADAM BROWN
WILLIAM BAIRD
FRANCIS BRODY } Baillies,
JAMES CLELAND

GEORGE WARRANDER Dean of Guild,
GAVIN PLUMMER Thefaurer,

And the Remanent Members of the Honourable Council of the Antient City of

EDINBURGH,

Right Honourable,

SEeing the Laws Authorize, and your Inclinations lead you to Check growing *Impiety* and *Superftition*, there is no
other

( )

other Person or Society, to whom the following Essay can be so properly Dedicated by,

Right Honourable,

Your Lordship's and Honours most Humble and Obedient Servant,

W. B.

THE

PREFACE.

THE three great Enemies of Religion, are *Deiſm*, *Libertiniſm*, and *Superſtition*, (for it is very juſtly doubted, if there be ſuch an Animal in Nature, as a ſpeculative *Atheiſt* ſtrictly ſo taken) The chief riſe whereof ſeems to be from Miſtaken Notions of the *Deity* : Each Man forming to himſelf a GOD, after his own Humour: The Lazy and Voluptuous imagine a Superior Power, without Providence, immerſ'd in the Joys of Heaven, fully ſatisfy'd in himſelf, nor cares he tho' the Inferior World go at ſixes and ſevens, thus the *Deiſt*

*

draws

draws a Picture of himself, and shows what he would do, were he Master of Omnipotence.

So *Lucretius,*

Omnis enim per se Divum natura necesse 'st
Immortali ævo summa cum pace fruatur,
Semota ab nostris rebus, sejunctaque longe ;
Nam privata dolore omni, privata periclis,
Ipsa suis pollens opibus, nihil indiga nostri,
Nec bene promeritis capitur, nec tangitur ira.

Thus Engl. by*Creech.*

For whatsoe'er's Divine must live in Peace,
In undisturb'd and everlasting ease :
Not care for us, from Fears and Dangers free,
Sufficient to its own Felicity :
Nought here below, nought in our Power it needs;
Ne're smiles at good, ne're frowns at Wicked Deeds.

The *Libertine* frames to himself a GOD all of Mercy, without the least regard to his Justice, which is an Attribute, he hath no mind to think on,
least

lest it should disturb him in the Fruition of his Lusts : he hardens himself more and more in his Wickedness, presuming upon that abused Attribute of his Maker, and the long sufferance of GOD, but renders him more secure, according to that of the *Psalmist : These things hast thou done, and I kept silence : thou thoughtest that I was altogether such an one as thy self* : But GOD will awake against them, and make them know, that they shall certainly be reckoned with, for all their Misdeeds : As in the latter part of the Verse; *but I will reprove thee, and and set them in order before thine eyes.* Psal. 50. verse 21.

Again the poor Superstitious Bigot Represents to himself, a Melancholy Scene of the Justice of GOD, without any consideration of his Mercy : He imagines a Cruel Tyrannical Power, delighting in the Torment, Destruction, and Ruine of his Creatures: And therefore shapes to himself a Worship suitable to the Notion he intertains of the *Deity* : Hence the Barbarous Human Sacrifices, in use among the *Heathens*, Sacrificing Children to *Moloch*, &c. And hence the Whippings, cutting of the Flesh, Extravagant Fastings, and other Voluntary Pennances, so much practised by the *Pagans, Mahometans*, and *Romish Votaries.* There is another kind of Super-

stition

ftition has its Rife from Pride: This kind of Hypocrite, not fatisfied with what Form of Worfhip GOD hath prefcribed in his Word, muft be making Additions of his own, but let thefe Menders of GOD'S Prefcriptions mind the threatning in the 29 Chap. of Ifaiah, v. 13, and 14. *Forasmuch as this People draw near me with their mouth, and with their Lips do honour me, but have removed their heart far from me, and their fear towards me is taught by the Precept of Men: Therefore behold, I will proceed to do a marvelous work amongft this People, even a Marvelous Work and a Wonder: for the wifdom of their wife Men fhall perifh, and the underftanding of their prudent Men fhall be hid.* But to proceed,

That *Roman Catholicifm* is a Patch-Work of *Jewifh* and *Heathen Ceremonies,* is fo certain, that their moft Famous Doctors confefs it; tho' the Mifchief is, they are fo far from mending, that they undertake to defend it (a) for the Author of the *Canon Confecrationem,* Reprefenting the *Jewifh* Ceremonies obferved in the Confecration of the Tabernacle, and Veffels thereof, reafons thus, *If the Jews which ferved to the fhaddow of the Law did thefe things,*
much

(a) *Decree of Gratian Part* 3. *Dift.* 1.

much more ought wee to do them, wee to whom the Grace
is manifested, which is given by JESUS CHRIST.
The *Glos* Argues yet better, *if the* Pagans did this, *how
much more ought we to do it ?* And *Baronius* is not a-
shamed to Write, that the Heathen Ceremonies have
been sanctified by the Christians. And tho' these Doctors were silent, the thing it self would speak. Is
not the whole Papal Hierarchie borrowed from the
Jews ? Who had their *Hhigh-Priest,* *Sacrificers,* their
Levites, and yet among them divers Orders and
Functions : And from the *Pagans,* who had their
Great-pontifs, Little-pontifs, Flamins, Arch-flamins,
and *Pro-flamins.* The Author of the Canon De-
creets acknowledgeth it, in the first part of the Decree of *Gratian* *Dist.* 1. and 21. and *Polidore Virgil
de inventoribus rerum Lib.* 4. *C.* 5. who likeways con-
fesseth, that the *Romish* Priests have borrowed of the
Jewish most part of their sacred habites, and that it
is evident enough, that the Institution is rather *He-
braical* than *Apostolick* ; And that they therein also i-
mitat the *Pagans. Ibid. L.* 4. *C.* 5. 7. Decree of *Gratian Part.* 1. *Dist.* 21.

The Fasts of four times, or *Ember days* were also Originally *Jewish,* as is Ingenuously acknowledged by the Author of the *Canon Jejunium quarti. Po-*

li-

Iidore Virgil says they were borrow'd of the Heathens. *De inv, rerum l. 6. C. 3.*

The Ch. of *Rome* owns she hath borrowed the manner of building and Consecrating Temples from the *Jews.* See the *Canon Consecrationem* ; But says, she hath also the Praise of *Paganism* therefore ; And cites the example of *Nebuhadnezar*, who invited all the great ones of his Kingdom to the Dedication of his Image of Gold, *Durand Ration. Divin. Offic. l. 1. C. 6. n. 2.*

Their Processions falsly attribute to *Pope Agapet*, were institute by *Numa Pompilius* (above a Thousand years before that *Pope* mounted the Chair) and called by him Supplication : Either to appease the wrath of the Gods, to obtain Peace, or to Pray to the Gods for the Fruits of the Earth, perform'd after this manner, first, some young Children, next the Sacrificing Priests in white Surplices, singing Hymns, Pæans and Canticles, to the Honour of their Gods, after them the High Priest or Curio : Then the *Roman Senators* with their Wives and Children and sometimes the common People assisted. The shrine or reliquary of *Jupiter* or *Anubis* was commonly carried about in the Procession, by some Priest in a white Surplice, wearing a Crown on his shaven-head. The Emperour and *High Pontif Commodus Antonius*

got

got his head fhaven round, exprefly to carry the Cabinet of the GOD *Anubis* : A Taper bearer with his Taper burning, went before the reliquary, feats were erected in the ftreets at convenient diftances, where the relique carriers-might reft and take Breath. When the Proceffion was ended, the Temples were opened, the Altars and Images perfumed with infence, and the reliques of their GODS, expof'd to the view of the People; nor did they want their *Hoftiæ Ambervales* in their Proceffions.

On Proceffion day a Feaft was celebrate, no fhops were opened, the hall of Juftice was fhut, and the Prifoners were unfettered : In fhort they obferved almoft all the fame ceremonies, which the *Papifts* do on *Corpus Chrifti day.* From all which it plainly appears, that the *Roman Catholicks* (as they call themfelves) have been carefully inftructed from Father to Son in the *Pompilian Religion.* See alfo the Proceffion of *Babylon* in the 6. *Ch.* of *Baruc.* Their GODS carried on fhoulders, the fhorn Priefts who cryed in carrying them; the people who went before and behind, and Worfhiped, a livley Image of the modern Proceffions. But as to the *Popes* making his GOD be carried on a white Hackney, the day of the moft Solemn Proceffion, while himfelf

is

isProudly Born on the shoulders of the most Honourable men in the City, and his carrying the same GOD among his baggage, when he takes a Journey with his Cardinals, there can be no example brought from antiquitie ; for never was there so wretched a *Pagan*, who did not render more Honour to his GOD, than the *Pope* yieldeth to what he seems to own for his maker and *SAVIOUR*.

Yet they may plead greater antiquitie for their Crowned bald-pates, and white Surplices ; for besides the *Priests* of the Goddess *Isi*, the Antient *Ægyptian Idolaters* used them. Under the Law the contrair was observed, nay they were forbid. *Levit. C. 19. v: 27. To round the Corners of their heads, and mar the Corners of their Beards. Ezek. C. 44. v: 20. Or shave their heads.* In the Gospel, they find no such Ceremonies commanded ; so you may guess whence they have them. For the addition of Cross or Banner in the *Procession*, the *Roman Idolaters* had their *Labarum*, a Sacred Ensign much Reverenced. *Antenor* pictured in it a Sow, from the Name *Troja*, in the Vulgar *Italian* a Sow, he Dedicated it to *Juno* Queen of the Heavens, because the Sow was the beloved *Victim* of that Goddess. Afterwards the *Romans* painted a Mercurie's *Caduce* on the Banner : And lastly an *Eagle* for the Ensign of the *Roman Em-*

The PREFACE.

Empire, with a staff set cross-way at the upper end of the Spear.

A little before the coming of CHRIST, a sect sprung up among the *Jews* called *Essenes*, *Saints*, because they affected a particular Austerity, and Holiness of Life ; They Lived a part in *Confraternities*, no Infants were receiv'd into their Orders, but only Men of ripe Age, and they, not till after some Years of probation. The *Initiat* brought in all his Goods, no Man possessed any thing in proper, they Lived all in *Common*, their Repast was in *Common*, their Chambers opened to none, who was not of their Sect, and the most part voluntarly abstained from Marriage. *See Josephus de Bello Jud. lib.* 10. *C.* 7. *Polidore Virgil* holdeth this to be the original of Monastick Life, only he observed, the *Monks* of *Rome* came not near the Holiness of the *Essenes* : For they (saith he) have for the most part their Tables *Royally* covered : They plunge themselves in Delights, purchase Honours, and Insatiably desire the Riches of the World. *De inv. rerum L.* 7. He might have added, the *Essenes* Lived not Idly as the *Monks*, for each of them had a Trade, and got his Living by the Labour of his Hands, before the rising of the Sun they gave themselves to Meditation, but soon

as

* *

as he returned to chear their eyes, they applyed themselves to Labour : Instead of eating the Goods of the Poor, they gave Alms : their Word was as good as their Oath ; they bound not themselves by Vow, never to Marry, nor fear'd they, that Wedlock was Sacriledge, and, a defiling ; for their Abstinence from it was Voluntar. But to proceed,

The *Jewish* Church had a *Holy-Oyle*, with which the Tabernacle and Vessels thereof, their Kings and Priests were Anointed. To be even with the *Jews*, the Church of *Rome* hath diverse sorts of Oyls, which she consecrateth with Prayers, and horrible Conjurations. With them, she Anoints *Temples, Altars, Chalices, Princes, Popes, Bishops, Priests, Deacons*, &c. This *Drug* is likewayes used in *Baptism, Confirmation*, and *Extreme Unction. See Polidore Virgil de inv. rerum L.* 5. *C.* 3.

The *Jewish* Church had certain Waters for the Legal purification, and the *Heathens* had their *Lustrate* ; So the Church of *Rome* must have her Spiritual Brine, or pickle against the *Devil* (her *Holy Water*) to put away *Venial Sins*, and drive out Ill Spirits, on which read the *Canon Aqua*, and as the *Jewish Priests* washed before they applyed themselves to the Sacrifices, so the washing of *Priests*, is one of the Ceremonies that goes before the *Mass. Polid. Virgil*

The PREFACE,

Virgil de invent. rerum Lib. 5. *C.* 10. From the same spring is the custom of burning Incense on the Altar.

The *Jews* Celebrate their Passover with Unleavened Bread, so the Church of *Rome*, will not Celebrate the *Eucharist* with Leavened Bread. the *Jews* had Lamps which enlightened the Night in the Tabernacle, the Church of *Rome* Light's Candles and Torches Night and Day in their Churches. In the *Jewish* Church, there was a Vail which covered the most Holy Place, so the Church of *Rome* in *Lent* covereth her Images with White Linnen. As the High Priest had little Bells fast'ned to the Hem of his Garment, of which he made the Sound to be heard, when he entered into, or departed from the Holy Place, so the Priests have their little Bells, which they found, when they elevate that which they call GOD; Also when they carry it to Sick Persons, or when they return from them.

In short, by little and little, they have burthen'd the Poor Church, with the Yoke of *Jewish* Ceremonies, contrar to the express Command of the *Apostle*, *Acts* 15. *v.* 10. *Why tempt ye GOD, to put a yoke upon the neck of the Disciples, which neither our Fathers, nor we were able to bear?* Our SAVIOUR JESUS CHRIST, who is the Body and Truth of all the

* * 2 Shad-

Shadows and Figures of the *Mofaical Law*, hath by his own proper Blood, abolithed all thofe Ordinances, and fixed them to his *Crofs*, according to the faying of the *Apoftle*, *Colof*: 2. *v*. 14. *Blotting out the Hand-writing of Ordinances, that was againft us, which was contrary to us, and took it out of the way, nailing it to his Crofs.* But the Church of *Rome* not content to re-patch the Vail of *Ceremonies*, which CHRIST JE-SUS hath torn by his Death; hath thereto fowed all forts of pieces and patches, which fhe hath borrowed of Antient *Paganifm*: And indeed, it is of the *Pagans*, that fhe Learn'd to join the Spiritual Power with the Temporal.

Our SAVIOUR refufed to divide the Inheritance between two Brothers, whence it is plain, he did not on Earth Exercife any Power, or Jurifdiction Temporal; But the Heathen Emperours joined both Powers together, qualifying themfelves for the moft part, *Emperours and Soveraign Pontifs*; fo the *Pope* boafts of both the Swords, holding that CHRIST hath given him both the Earthly and Heavenly Empire, to manifeft, that this is the Beaft, to which the Dragon, *viz.* The Heathen Empire gave his Throne. *Rev.* 13. *v.* 2.

The *Pagans* when they confecrated a Soveraign Pontif, Adored and Worfhipped him, fo when a

Pope

Pope is chosen, they set him on the Altar, and all the *Cardinals* go to Adoration.

The Emperour *Domitian* made himself to be called our LORD GOD, (*) so the *Pope* calleth himself GOD in a Letter to the Emperour. *par.* 1. *Dist.* Gr. 96. *C.* 7. Wherein speaking of his Exemption from Secular Powers, he saith GOD (meaning himself) cannot be Judged by Men.

It is from the Antient *Pagans*, the *Popes* learned to make Men kiss their Feet. Our SAVIOUR washed the Feet of his *Apostles, John* 13. *v.* 14. But the Soveraign *Pontifs* among the *Pagans* made their Feet to be kissed ; so *Dioclesian* ordained by a publick Edict, that all persons should prostrate themselves before him, and kiss his Feet. And to make them the more venerable, he adorned and enriched his *Pantofle* with Gold, Pearls, and Precious-stones. Another Monster of Nature, *C. Caligula* before him manifested the same Pride. *Seneca de benef. lib.* 2. *c.* 12. For after he had absolved *Pompeius Pennus,* he stretcht him out his left Foot, to kiss it, altho' he was a *Consul.*

It is also of the *Pagans* the Pope hath Learn'd to have himself carried on Mens Shoulders. *Juvenal, Martial.*

The

(*) *Sueton.*

The PREFACE.

The Antient *Pagans* acknowledged one GOD, who had the univerſal Empire over all Creatures, but beſides, they Worſhipped an infinite number of *Gods, Demi-gods,* and *Goddeſſes* ; ſo the Church of *Rome* conſeſſeth there is one Soveraign GDD, Creator of all Things, and that he hath no Companion ; yet beſides him there are many *Hee-Saints,* and *Shee-Saints,* to whom ſhe yieldeth Divine Honours.

And as the *Pagans* among their, *Shee-Gods* had one whom they called the *Queen of Heaven* ; ſo beſides the numberleſs *Shee-ſaints,* the Church of *Rome* hath one to whom many give the Title of *Goddeſs,* and which almoſt all acknowledge for the *Queen of Heaven,* and *Lady of the World.* Never was *Juno, Veſta, Minerva, Ceres, Diana,* or *Venus,* who as the Poet *Ennius* reckons, were *Heathen Shee-Gods of the Upper-Houſe,* more fiducially invock'd, or ſo ſolemnly courted by the *Pagan,* as the *Virgin Mary* is by the now *Roman Church* : *ſee her Offices.*

And as one and the ſame *God* was diverſly nam'd, according to the places where he was Worſhipped, or the Effects which were aſcrib'd unto him, as *Jupiter Ammon, Jupiter Olympien, Jupiter Stator, Jupiter Ultor, Jupiter Victor, Jupiter Conſervator, Jupiter Feretrein,* &c. So the Church of *Rome* hath *Our Lady of Loretta, Our Lady of Montſerrat, Our Lady the Ægyptian,*

yptian, *Our Lady of Joy*, *Our Lady of Good News*, *Our Lady of Recovery*, *Our Lady of the Annunciation*, *Our Lady of Fevers*, *Our Lady of deliver us from the pains of Hell*, &c.

And as the *Heathens* had their *Little-Gods* which always went by pairs as *Castor* and *Pollux*, so hath the Church of *Rome* her *Little Saints*, which never walk alone, as *St. Cosme*, and *St. Damain*, none could be publickly Worshipped among the Old *Romans*, who was not Deified by the Senate of *Rome*, nor may any be invoked or served by the Modern *Romans*, who hath not been Cannonised by the *Pope* and *Cardinals*, who are the Senators of New *Rome*, and as the Pagans Assigned particular Offices to their *Gods*, as *Neptune* ruled over the Waters, *Æolus* over the Winds, *Ceres* preserv'd the Corn, and *Bachus* had care of the Wine, the Soldiers followd *Mars*, Men of Learning addressd themselves to *Minerva*, Poets invocked *Apollo*, and the *Physicians Æsculapius*, Mariners had their refuge to *Neptune*, *Hunters* implored the favour of *Diana*, *Vulcan* was the *God* of the Smiths, *Pan* of the Shepherds, and *Mercury* of Merchants, &c. so hath the Church of *Rome* distributed to every *Saint* his Office and Charge, The Idolatry is the same, tho' the persons are changed: *Janus* hath left his Keys to St. *Peter*, *Lucina* resign'd

her

her care of Child-bed Women to St. *Margaret*: for Rain, they no more Addreſs themſelves to *Jupiter Pluvius* but to *St. Genivieve*: St. *George* a Horſe-back hath ſupplanted *Mars*: *St. Katharine* preſides over the Sciences in place of *Minerva*: the Phyſicians no more follow *Æſculapius,* but St. *Coſme,* and St. *Damian*: Seamen invoke *St. Nicolas* inſtead of *Neptune*: and *Hunters* have abandoned *Diana* to follow St. *Euſtace,* and St. *Hubert,* &c. nay they have their Canting Saints too, as St. *Gotard* for the *Gout* St. *Lucie* for *ſore Eyes,* and becauſe in Italian *Matto* ſignifies a Fool, they recommend the Fools to St. *Mathurin*: becauſe moſt Records, Sciences, &c. were Written, and moſt Books Printed in Latine, the Secretaries .and Printers have choſen St. *John Porte-Latin* for their Saint: The Roaſting-cooks would have no other than the *Virgin-Mary* for their *Goddeſs,* and moſt devoutly celebrate the Feaſt of her Aſſumption, becauſe *Aſſum* hath a ſignification of Roaſting: The Looking-glaſs and Speƈticle-makers do homage to St. *Claire*: the *Paviers* Worſhip *St. Roc*: becauſe *Eloy* in the Greek ſignifies *Nails,* St. *Eloy* is the Patron of the *Smiths*: St. *Creſpin* is the Favorite of the *Shoe-Makers,* becauſe *Crepida* is Latin for a *Pantofle*: the Scavengers call on St. *Fiacre,* becauſe of the goodly correſpondence of the Name.

Among

The PREFACE,

Among the Antient Pagans every Country, City yea every Family had their Tutelar God, as *Dagon* was the *God* of the *Philistines*, *Astorat* of the *Sidonians*, *Molec* of the *Ammonites*, *Hemos* of the *Moabites*, *Astartes* of the *Syrians*, *Diasercs* of the *Arabians*, *Romulus* of *Rome*, and *Apollo* of *Delphos*, *Carthage* was under the Protection of *Juno*, *Athens* of *Minerva* and *Cyprus* of *Venus*, &c. That the Ch. of *Rome* might be in nothing behind the Heathens excepting name only, she hath for several Countries, Citys, &c. Patrons, Guardians, Tutelar Genii, Demons, Heroes or what you please to call them, as St. *Denis* for *France*, St. *Martin* for *Germany*, St. *Peter* and *Paul* for *Rome*, St. *James* for *Spain*, St. *Mary* for *Switzerland*, St. *Patrick* for *Ireland*, St. *Andrew* for *Scotland*, St. *George* for *England*, St. *Mark* for *Venice*, St. *Geneviev* for *Paris*, &c. Nay ev'ry City or Village speed as well among them, yea particular Arts, and their dear Whores too. And for particular Cattel as Oxen, sheep the very geese they have their Saints, and which by no means may be forgotten, *St*· *Antony* must be Prayed to as patron of the Hogs. *According to the Number of thy City's were thy Gods, O Judah; and according to the Number of the streets of Jerusalem, have ye set up Altars to that shamefull thing.* *Jerem. C.* 11. *v.* 13.

* * *

And

And as the Pagans tho they believ'd their Gods dwelt in an Heavenly Palace, yet reprefented them on Earth by an Infinite company of Images ; which they had in great Honour : Plac'd them in their Temples, fet them on the Altars, faftned them in crofs-ways : Yea fome they Cloathed in Magnifi-cent Habits, Crowned with Flowers, and carried in Proceffions on the fhoulders of their fhaven Priefts. So the Ch. of *Rome* tho fhe believeth her Saints are in Heaven ; yet muft have her Images thefe *Bartholomew Babies* muft have Religious Wor-fhip pay'd to them ; muft be placed in Temples, fe on Altars, faftened in crofs-ways and on the Gates o Citys : Candles are lighted to them, Pilgrimage vowed to them, they are painted and Crowned with Flowers, Priefts carry them in Proceffion o their fhoulders, the people fall on their knees be fore them, &c. In fhort all the Idolatries practifed by the *Pagans* of old in the place of the Images o their falfe *Gods*, are now practif'd by the Ch. o *Rome*, in the place of the Images of her *Sts.* Th Antient *Pagans* Confecrated Temples and Altars t their *Gods*, fo doth the Ch. of *Rome* to the *Saint* And as the *Pagan Gods* have quitted to the *Saints* th Protection of Kingdoms, &c. So have they to then refigned their Magnificent Temples and ftate Altars. Fo

The PREFACE,

For *Platina* faith, the Barbarous Tyrant and Ufurper *Phocas* (that flew his Mafter after he had Deftroyed his Emprefs, and her five Sons, before his Face, to make his way through Innocent Blood to the Crown) gave leave to *Boniface* the 4t. to Confecrate in Honour to the Virgin *Mary* and all the *Martyrs*, the *Pantheon*, a Temple fo called becaufe it was Dedicated to all the *Gods*, and their Mother *Cybelle* : The fame hath been practifed concerning the other Temples; for what before were Confecrated to *Saturn, Jupiter, Mars, Apollo, Juno, Minerva,* and *Venus,* &c. Are now Dedicated to St. *Adrian,* S. *Mary* of Pains of Hell, S. *Mary* of Fevers, S. *Petronilla,* S. *Lawrence,* S. *Mary* of *Minerva,* S. *Barba,* &c. The *Pagans* Confecrated Feaft days to their *Gods,* fo hath the Ch. of *Rome* Dedicated them to her *Saints.* And as on the Feaft days of the *Pagans,* the Priefts were Crowned with Flowers, and the Gates of the Temples were Adorned with Laurel, &c. Such is the Ornament of the Feafts of *Rome,* and namely of the Jubile : For all the Gates and ftations are Invironed with Green Bufhes, &c.

In the *Pagan* Feafts it was exprefly forbidden to labour, and thofe that wrought were punifh'd, tho it was permitted to play, dance, and commit all forts of Infolencies : So in the Popifh Feafts, if a poor

man

man work in his shop to relieve his languishing Family, he is sure to be severely punished, though the
Law of GOD says, *six days shalt thou Labour* ; But into Taverns stews and other shameless places, he may
enter without the least Censure or rebuke ; it is then
that the Priests and people make merry ; and commit the greatest excess of Gluttony and Drunkenness,
see, *Polidore Virgil. L.* 5. *C.* 1. & 2. Who acknowledgeth, this custom is from the Antient *Romans.*
hath not the Follies and Masques of the Carnival or
shrove-tide succeeded to the *Bachanals*, or at least to
that idle Feast which the *Pagans* Celebrate to their
great *Goddess* : For at that time every on had Liberty to pass the time in all sort of Insolencies, to go
in Masque, and in what Habit they would. There
was no Magistrate, no dignity so great, or Honourable, to whom it was not permitted to change habits.
Hath not the Feast of the three Kings succeeded to
the *Saturnals*. *Baptista Mantuan Fastorum. L.* 8. *Plu-
tarchs* Life of *Romulus.*

So the Feast of Innocents hath succeeded the *Lu-
percales*. After Sacrifice was kill'd, they brought two
Children, Noblemens *Sons* whose fore-heads some
of the *Luperci* stained with the Bloody knife, while
others wiped it off with locks of wooll dip'd in Milk ;
the Boys were oblidged to laugh after their fore-heads
were

were wip'd. And having cut the Goat's skin into thongs, the Boys run about the streets all naked but their midle beating all they met in their Proceffion. The young Women were content to be beat, thinking it would make them Conceive, and be Happily Deliveted : And no doubt thofe whips had then the fame virtue that *St. Margarets* girdle has, at this day. The Feaft of the Chair of *St. Peter* (according to the Bifhop of *Mande*) (*) Was Antiently called the Feaft of the Banquet of *St. Peter* becaufe it fucceeded a *Pagan* Feaft in which the poor Idolaters offered to GOD Wine and Meat on the Tombs of their Parents. So the Feaft of the Bonds of *St. Peter* fucceeded a Feaft of the Chain of Gold of the Emperour *Auguftus*: as the fame doctor contefleth. *Ration. Div. Offic. L.* 7. *C.* 19. The Antient *Romans* in the beginning of *February* Celebrated the Feaft of the Purification of *Febra*, Mother of *God Mars*, and in the Honour of this *Goddefs* they lighted Torches and Lamps. But *Pope Sergius* ordained this Feaft of the Purification fhould be Celebrated in Honour of the Virgin *Mary* (whether he knew the Blefled Virgin took pleafure to be ferv'd after the *Pagan* fafhion is a queftion) and that the people fhould go through the Churches with Torches and candles in their hands, fee *Durand. Rat. Divin. Offic. L.* 7. *C.* 7. When

(*) *Durand. Ration. Div. Offic. L.* 7. *C.* 8.

The PREFACE.

When the *Pagan Priests* were confecrated, they made a Solemn Banquet, as may be feen in *Apulee's* Golden *Afs*. *Polydore Virgil* faith, thence cometh the cuftom, that the Priefts when they fing their firft Mafs, make a Feaft, and invite their fellow Priefts and Friends to drink of the Theological Wines. There was nothing more delicious, or magnificient then the Supper made after the Confecration of the Chief *Pagan Pontif*, to which has fucceeded the Feaft, made after the Coronation of the *Pope*, with this difference, that the *Emperour* fhould hold Water to the *Pope*, and Kings are placed below *Cardinals*: *Pagan* Antiquity never faw fuch a Monfter of Pride.

The Church of *Rome* hath her Convents of *Nuns* in imitation of the *Roman Veftals*, fo called from the *Shee-God Vefta*, to whom they were Confecrated; and in whofe Temple they dwelt. They were much honoured and efteemed for their Sanctity among the *Romans*. when they were initiat, they were fhaven as the *Nuns*, at this day: rhey took a Vail and were reinvefted with long White Robes, the entry of their Houfes were forbidden to Men, as that of the Reformed Monaftry of the *Nuns*, they had publick Rents and Revenues, Wealthy People, on Deathbed, left them Legacies: and as the *Nuns* have their

Ab-

Abbefs, who commands them ; fo had they their Governefs, who was called *Maxima.* among the Veftals, were little *Nuns,* brought there in their Infancy, for they were admitted betwixt fix and ten years : fo are the *Romifh Nunries* full of Infants and young Maids : But one notable difference there is, that during the firft Ten years, the Veftals were only Novices, during other Ten, they applyed themfelves to the Service and Sacrifice, and other Ten, they taught the young *Nuns,* fo at the end of Thirty Years they were permitted to Marry ; Wherefore the *Pagans* will rife in Judgement with the Church of *Rome,* and condemn her of the Tyranny fhe Exercifeth towards poor Girls, who being lured or forced into a Convent, can never go out again, no more than the Fifh can out of the net. And what are the confequences of this conftrained celibacy *Nicolaus de Clemangus* one of the Doctors of *Paris* and Arch-Deacon of *Baion* upwards of 200 years ago hath told us in thefe words, *de corrupto ftatu Ecclef: C. 23. Quid obfecro aliud funt hoc tempore puellarum Monafteria nifi quædam, non dico Dei Sanctuaria, fed veneris exfecranda proftibula ; fed lafcivorum & impudicorum quædam ad libidines explendas receptacula ? ut idem fit hodie puellam velare quod publice ad fcortandum exponere.* What I pray you are the prefent Monaftries

of

of young Women, other than, I fay not Sanctuaries of GOD, but curfed ftews of *Venus*, but receptacles of Lafcivious young Whore-Mafters, for the gratifying of their Lufts? So that, at this day to put a Maid into a *Nunnery* is juft the fame with entering her into a publick Whore-houfe.

It is in imitation of the *Pagans* that the *Monks* Difcipline themfelves, and that there are Confraternities of Whippers, GOD forbad, his people to make incifion in their Flefh, *Levit.* 19. *v.* 28. But the Priefts of *Baal* cut themfelves with Knives till the Blood came, 1 *Kings* 18. v. 28. And the Priefts of *Cybele* Whipped, and lacerated themfelves, till the Blood run down: This produced abundance of Money from the good people, who pityed them, with which they made merry in fecret, *See Apulæ* in his Golden *Afs.*

At the fame School the Church of *Rome* Learned to build her Altars to the Eaft, and their Priefts, to turn themfelves that way, when they offer their Sacrifices.

As the great *Pagan Pontif* confecrated little Images of *Jupiter's* Thunder-bolt, which the poor Idolater Worfhipped, and believed there was virtue in them, againft Lightnings and Tempefts; So the Pope in in the firft year of his Popefhip, and every

seventh

seventh year after, while he liveth, useth to Conse-crate The *Agnus Dei (a)* after this manner; when they are presented to him in Boxes, he, dressed up in all his *Pontificalibus* sets about a most Prophane *Paganish*, and plain *Conjurers* Baptisme of the same. they call it Consecration.

And first the Water, in some great Vessel there, prepared, is charmed by pouring Balsom and Chrisme crossways into it, and Pronouncing two or three *Spells*; so the Water being Charmed enough by this time, the *Pope* turns him to the Boxes, off goes his Mitre, and to Conjuring again falls he : and lest this should not do the feat, there is a second Charm with three Crosses, all of them too long to be Transcribed; and a third with as many according to the true Rule of Witchery.

Virg. Eccl. 8   *Numero Deus impare gaudet.*

Unequal numbers please the God.

Then the *Pope* Baptizeth them, the Prelats take them out, put them in Basons of Silver, and carry them to the Tables to be dryed with clean Towels. And after two pretty long spells more, with five Crosses in them, to enable them against all Mischiefs of Men and Devils, and to help Women in Travel, and a-many other fine Jobbs, out comes an *Elixir Salutis*

* * * *

of

(a.) *Sacrar Cerem.* l. 1. C. 8.

of the Mafter Conjurers own Preparation, and with the Devils Acclamation thereunto ; *Probatum eft.*

Their Doctrine of *Purgatory,* is frcm the *Heathens* alfo, and *Bellarmine* proves, there is a *Purgatory, L. 1. C:7.de Purg.* from the Teftimony of *Plato, Cicero* and *Virgil.* He fays *Ibid. L. 1. C. 1.* it is a place (*no body knows where*) for there be *Ibid. L. 2. C. 6.* eight feveral opinions of it, and the Church hath not defined it : *But by the beft intelligence, 'tis in Utopia,* wherein, as in a prifon, Souls are Purged after this life, which were not fully purged in it : That being fo purged, they may be able to enter Heaven where nothing undefiled comes, but this whole fable which they borrow from *Virgil, Plato* and *Homer,* is not only all without Gods Book, but againft it fully. For as thereby the World is divided but into two parts, the Eleft and Reprobate, Believers and Unbelievers, in this life ; fo it fuitably affigns a double ftate, and no more, after it ; Namely, happinefs and Mifery, and both unchangeable and Eternal. *Mark C. 16. V. 16. He that believeth, and is Baptized, fhall be faved ; but he that believeth not, fhall be Damned. Math. C: 25. V: ult, John C. 3. V. 36. John C. 5, V, 29. Rom. C. 2. V. 6: 7: 8: 9.* And the examples of *Dives* and *Lazarus,* make plain Demonftration that the *Saints* after Death are prefently and for ever bleffed ; and
the

the Wicked are Miferable forthwith, and Eternally. *Luke* 16. and tho' the beft of Believers have the remains of fin till death, 1 *John* 1. *v.* 8. yet at it, they prefently pafs to Life, and blefs. 2 *Corinth.* 5. *v.* 1. 2. and are not lodged in the Suburbs of Hell, as Papifts teach, until redeemed by their Maffes, or fuch like Trumperies.

Praying for the Dead, was in ufe among the old *Pagans*, by which, and offering Sacrifices and a-many other Ceremonies they thought to leffen or lighten the Torments of the deceaf'd. Hence the Prayers, Singing of Maffes, ringing of Bells, &c. in the Church of *Rome* for the Dead. But thanks to Purgatory for this Doctrine, for were there no fuch *Little-eafe*, who would give a farthing for all the Sacrifices, Ringing of Bells, &c. in the World to prevent the going thither, or delivering thence? but the fearful Faith of that, will fetch out all the Money for this. And no doubt, it is well worthy of it, if the whole Colledge of Mountebanks, I mean the *Council of Trent*, *Seff.* 22. *C.* 2. have given a faithful account of the Virtues thereof. 'Tis offered, fay they, not only for the Sins, Punifhments, and *Satisfactions*, and other Neceffities of the Faithful Living; but alfo for the Dead in CHRIST not throughly purged yet: That is to fay, whofe Lodging is in

* * * * 2 the

the *Little-eafe* of Purgatory. And as on the ninth Day after the Death the *Pagans* ufed a Solemn Service, during which they magnificently entertain'd the Priefts of the falfe *Gods* : So in the Church of *Rome* feven Days after the deceafe, they do the Service of the Dead; and while the Friends of the Defunct are Weeping, the Jolly Priefts Sing and make Merry. Hence the *Canon* whereby the Priefts are forbid to be in Heavinefs, when they Celebrate the Service of the Dead.

And as the *Pagans*, befides the particular Service for every Dead Perfon, had alfo their Annual Feafts deftinated, to Celebrate the Memories of the Dead. So the Church of *Rome* to be nothing behind with them, doth every year Celebrate the Feaft of the Dead : The People crouding into the Churchyards, ftriving, who fhall mumble out moft Prayers, *&c.*

The Church of *Rome* boafteth much of her Miracles. So not only *Hereticks* and *Turks* have pleaded Miracles as well as they, but very *Heathens* can make as fair a claim to GOD by this kind of Argument as themfelves. And if the *Romanifts* never ftick to Damn, as Devilifh, the *Heathen* wonders ; their own, being fo much like them, may be juftly Judged by Proteftants, to be of the felf fame breed. I

fhall

shall be at a little pains in making the comparifon betwixt the Heathenifh and Popifh wonders: The former whereof both for their feeming excellency, and credibility alfo, may fairly vie before Impartial Judges with the latter.

First then *Vefpafian's* making the blind-man fee, by fpitting on his Cheeks and eyes, and the lame-man found by kicking him with his foot, *(b)* Are wonders not inferior to *Bernards* blind woman cured by the fign of a crofs, *(c)* And *Cuthberts* Lady made to walk, by fprinkling of his Holy Water, *Ciefevs Ch: Hift. lib.* 19. C. 7.

Again, That *Servius Tullius,* whilft a little Child and fleeping, fhould have Flames of Fire fparkling about his head, *(d)* Will match, I trow, the ftar, St. *Dominick's* God-mother in a Night Vifion, faw upon his forehead in his Infancy: *Vinc. Spec. Hift. L.* 29. C. 94.

So the Child of fix Moneths age, proclaiming a Triumph in the Ox-market at *Rome,* *(e)* is every-whit as noteable a Feat as *Pope Sergius's* reputed baftard's clearing him, that was called his Father, from being a whor-mafter, *Baron. Annal. Anno* 699. *n.* 2.   Xer-

(b) *Tacit Hift. Book* 4 *near the end.* (c) *Miracula J. Bern. C.* 15. (d) *Valerius Maximus lib.* 1. *de fervio Tullo.* (e) *Val. Max. lib.* 1. *de C. volum & ferv. fulpit.*

Xerxes's Wine, that being poured into his Goblet was once, again, and a third time turned into Blood ; (*f*) looks bigger far than the Priests Water wherein he wash'd his Fingers after Confecration, that was ferved fo ; *Barron. Ann.* Anno 1192 *n.* 2.

Nay the Apparition to *Auguftus's* Phyfitian in his Dream, that forbad the General's abfence from the Battel to be fought next day, altho he were fick ; and whereupon being carried out in a Litter he fcaped the Enemies hands who took his Camp, (*g*) is as Authentick a Revelation, as *St. Peter's Paul's* and *Andrew's* Saluting *Dunftan* in his Sleep. when *Peter* flapt him with a ferula on the hand for refufing a Bifhoprick, which made him learn more wit againft the next opportunity. (*h*)

Moft certain the Heathen and *Roman Divi,* or *Saints,* feem equally intent upon rewarding and punifhing people, as their Worfhip was obferved or neglected by them. For as *Hercules* cut off thirty of the *Potitii*; whom he had Affigned to his Service, within one years time for fubftituting flaves

to

(*f*) *Val. Max. lib.* 1. *de equa pariente Leporem.* (*g*) *Val. Max. lib.* 1. *de Somniis.* (*h*) *Creffy* Ch. Hift. lib. 31. C. 25.

to Minister to him, and took away the fight of *Appius* that put them on fo doing ; (*ı*) *So Dunstan* knock'd on the head, the poor *Monk* that was about to forfake his Monaftery ; and fent his ficknefs unto him again, that fpoke flightly of the cure, fuppofed to be had from him, (*k*) and hundred's more like thefe.

And even as the Heathens faftned Tables in the Temple of the *God*, by whom they thought they were healed, and therein wrote the difeafes whereof they had been cured.

So the Ch of *Rome* afcribes to *Saints* all the cures which are done, and for a memorial Confecrates Infcriptions of them in the Churches and Chappels, as may be feen in all their places of Idolatry.

And as the *Pagans* offered to their *Gods* Images of Earth refembling the parts of their Bodies, fo the Superftitious of the Ch. of *Rome* offer Images of wax, of the fafhion of the hand, foot, or breaft which hath been healed : And as Superftition hath no bounds, the cuftom hath paffed from men to beafts : So that at this day they place in their Churches, the like Images of their Oxen, Horfes, and Sheep. *Polidore Virgil* approves this Superftition and calls it

Scru-

(*ı*) *Val. Max. lib.* 1. *de Potitio non obfervante Sacra.*
(*k*) *Vinc. Spec. Hift. lib.* 24. *C.* 96.

Scrupulous Bafhfulnefs to fear to imitate the _Pagans_ in this point ; _de invent rerum. L._ 5. _C._ 1.

The Ch. of _Rome_ ufeth alfo the fame reafons to defend her Superftitions which the Antient _Pagans_ ufed ; fo _Seneca_ excufeth _Caligula_ for offering his feet to be kiffed, faying it was not done through Infolence, but only to let them fee his pantofle inriched with Gold and Pearles ; (_l_) even fo the _Popes_ flatterers would make us believe it is not out of pride that he makes Kings and Princes kifs his feet, but in Honour of the crofs of Gold Embroidered on his flipper.

The Antient Chriftians reproach'd the Heathens with the multitude of their _Gods_ and deified men which they adored : The _Pagans_ anfwered the perfons they honoured were the Friends of GOD, and in honouring them they honoured GOD himfelf ; that thefe Bleffed Spirits carried the Prayers of men to GOD, that by the Creature they went to the Creator no otherwife than as one goes to the King by his Officers : Scarce a Child but knoweth thefe are the very excufes of the Ch. of _Rome_ when we reproach her with Saint Worfhip, tho the _Apoftle_ exprefly tells us, (_m_) there is but one Mediator betwixt GOD and Man, the Man CHRIST JESUS. Which very thing his LORD, and ours, had fpoken

in

(_l_) _De Benefic. l._ 2. _c._ 12. (_m_) 1 _Tim. c._ 2. _v:_ 5.

in effect before him, saying, *John* 14. *v.* 6. *no man cometh to the Father but by me.* And to conclude, the best Creatures, *Isaiah* 63. *v.* 16. cannot hear us, *Rev.* 19. *v.* 10. and *C.* 22. *v.* 9. Refuse Religious Worship from us : And there is not in the whole Scriptures one Example of such homage payed with Approbation.

When the *Pagans* were reproached with Worshipping of Images they protested, they honoured not the Image it self, but what it represented *Celsus ap. Origen. l.* 7. ev'n so doth the Church of *Rome* excuse her Idolatry. yet this is but the Modesty of a few : While others, and of greatest Authority and Credit among the *Romanists,* such as St. *Thomas,* St. *Bonaventure,* and Cardinal *Cajetan,* &c. Labour by seven Arguments to prove the same Worship due to the Image, and the Exemplar or Person represented by it. *As Bellarmine* shews us *de Imag. l.* 2. *C.* 20. and himself that would fain seem to be a third sort of Idolater, and in the mean betwixt two extreams, dodgeth apparently, and in effect shakes hands with the worser side. He Affirms that Images are properly, and by themselves to be Religiously Worshipped:but as to the same kind of Worship due to the Exemplar, with that indeed only improperly and by accident.

* * * * *

cident. Which you muſt think the vulgar in their
practiſe will very wiſely diſtinguiſh.

But notwithſtanding GOD'S word, and ſillineſs
of their Heatheniſh Excuſes, they will abide in their
Idolatry ; and prove it good to do ſo too, by Miracles forſooth. *Bellarmin* ſaith, *lib.* 2. C. 12. *de*
Imag. GOD by the Images of CHRIST and Saints,
works many Miracles : Whence we underſtand,
the Worſhipping of Images pleaſeth him. Very well
argued for a Cardinal ! But prey *Reader,* would
not this do as well. CHRIST wrought a great
Miracle by Clay and Spitle : *Ergo,* to Worſhip
Clay and Spitle would be pleaſing unto GOD. *Spe-*
ctatum admiſſi riſum ? Inſtances of thoſe Wonders
done by Images, you have enough there : But true
Miracles they cannot be, becauſe they ſerve a
curſed Lye, and maintain Idolatry.

I think it not amiſs to place the *Jubile* among the
Ceremonies, the Church of *Rome* hath borrowed of
Judaiſm and *Paganiſm. Platina* ſaith *Boneface* the 8 was
the Introducer of the *Jemiſh Jubile* among Chriſtians.
As for the *Pagan Jubile,* or ſæcular Plays firſt celebrated,
Anno A.U.C. 245, or 298, they were Celebrated every
hundreth Year, according to the common Opinion,
tho' the Ambitious Emperours afterwards deſirous
to have the Honour of Celebrating theſe Games in
their

their Reigns upon the flighteft pretence, many times made them return before their Ordinary Courfe. Thus *Claudius* pretended, that *Auguftus* held the Games before their due time, that he might have the leaft Excufe to keep them within fixty four years afterwards. On which account *Sueto-nius* tells us that the People fcoffed his Cryers, when they went about, Proclaiming Games, that no body had ever feen, nor would fee again. And *Polidore Virgil* faith *Pope Boniface* the 8 ordain'd a *Jubile* fhould be Celebrated every 100 Year ; which feemeth to be done to divert the People, and particularly the People of *Rome* from the vain fhow of the Secular Games, and to lead them to the true facred Solemni-tie : Tho' Clement the 6, and *Sixtus* the 4 willing to have part of the Glory and profite fhortned the time.

The Secular Plays were Celebrated in the City of *Rome,* fo is the *Jubile.*

Before the Secular Games began, the *Heraulds* invited the People to come and fee them. So the *Papal* (falfely called *Apoftolick*) *Trumpet* invites all the World to come to their *Jubile.*

The *Pagans* encourag'd People to come and fee their Games, telling them they fhould fee what they never had feen already, and fhould never fee again : So the *Popes* by their Bulls amplify the pretended Graces of their *Jubile.* And Reprefenting the fhortnefs of Life, invite all the World, not to let flip fo favourable an occafion.

Dureing the time of the Secular Plays, the poor Idolaters were promifed the Expiation, and Abolition of their Sins: So *Boniface* the 8 Declared, that whofoever now, would vi-fite the Threfhholds of the *Apoftles,* (that is St. *Peters* and *Pauls* Church at *Rome,*)fhould have the full Remiffion of all their Sins. Fairly offered at the firft opening of his *Shop* !

But

But Beginners muft allow good Pennyworths to force a Trade : Thefe Plenary Indulgences are ftill in ufe.

As the *Pope* doth now, fo did the *Emperour* then go in Proceffion to the Temples of the *Gods*.

At the beginning of the *Pagan Jubile*, they uncovered a certain Altar Dedicated to *Pluto* and *Proferpine*, which lay hid in the Earth till then, and the Plays were no fooner over, than they covered it again with Earth. So in *Rome* which calleth her felf *Chriftian*, there is a Gate called *Holy*, which is opened at the beginning of the *Jubile*, and fhut again as foon as the fame is ended. And it is remarkable the *Pope* opens it with a Silver Hammer, and leaves fome Pieces of Gold and Silver there before it is fhut again , as if he did ev'n at this Day Honour to the *God of Riches*. During the Secular Plays, they vifited the Temples, Altars, and Relicts, offered Sacrifices, and prefented Prayers to divers *Gods* and *Goddeffes*, the like is practifed in the *Papal Jubile*.

At every Solemnity they compofed new Hymns, fo at every *Jubile* new Prayers, *&c.*

They Graved on an Altar of Brafs under what *Conful* or *Emperour* the Plays were Celebrated, as the Modern *Romans* do under what *Pope*.

To conclude the Comparifon, as the *Emperours* being made Chriftians, Abolifhed thefe Games, *&c.* So I hope that Chriftian Kings and Princes, when GOD fhall give them Grace to take into confideration, the Superftition and Impiety of the *Romifh Whore* will deftroy her : For thofe who have given their Power and Authority to the Beaft, are thofe who fhall make her defolate and naked, and eat her flefh. *Rev. C.* 17.

Im-

Impiety *and* Superstition

EXPOSED:

A Poetical ESSAY.

Jude, part of the 4*th* Verse,

-------- *Ungodly men,* turning the Grace of our GOD into *Lasciviousness;* -----

TH' Impious quaff off Sin, ev'n till they burst,
  Each greedy draught, does but inflame their Thirst.
Ten Thousand Sins do but increase the Fire,
Ten Thousand more, they but provoke desire;
For Sin has always this attending curse,
To back the first Transgression with a worse.
How well does holy *Job* express this truth, *(a)*
That mischief's luscious in the Sinners mouth ;
And *Solomon* their folly does express, *(b)*
Who count it sport to act their Wickedness.

A

Mon-

(a) Chap: 20. Verse 12.   *(b)* Prov: 10. V: 23.

Monfters of Men, whence do'th your joy arife :
From Sin, which fhould to fountains turn your eyes ?
How long will ye your wife Reprovers mock ?
How long the Sin-Revenging GOD provock ?
In never dying Flames, can there be gain ?
Or is there pleafure in eternal pain ?
How do you imitate their folly, who,
Are ftill contracting Debt, where e'er they go ?
No thoughts they have, how to provide the Cafh ;
Or how to fhun the Laws impending Lafh ;
Still Carelefs they, they're in a Prifon thrown ;
Nor can they from that doleful place be gone,
Untill the utmoft farthing be paid down.
A Man you may deceive ; but here's the odd,
There's no deceiving the Omnifc'ent GOD.
Your Bond may perifh, Creditors will die,
But the Eternal GOD indures for ay.
Ungodly Men, and whence fo hard a name ?
They're void of Grace, no fear of GOD 's in them.
With Vice and Folly Stuft, what can be worfe ?
No ftate of Man can be a greater curfe.
For as the fear of GOD is Wifdoms head, *(c)*
Lifes fountain, and from fnares of Death doth lead. *(d)*
Even fo Ungodlinefs both gives the rife,
And is it felf the parent of all other Vice :

It,

(c) *Prov.* I. V: 7. (d) *Prov:* 14. V: 27.

It, it alone deprives Men of their Breath,
The fpring of Sp'ritual and Eternal Death.
So *Paul* bears Witnefs, that the Nations who (e)
Knew GOD, and yet on hm did not beftow
The Worfhip and the Reverence due; for this
He gave them up to ev'ry fordid Vice. *(f)*
This was the Spring, here was the Fountain head,
Hence all the num'rous Sins which in that place you Read.
This *Ab'ram* knew, and hence he did conclude, *(g)*
Abimelech would furely fpill his Blood
For *Sara's* fake, for where there is no fear
Of GOD, no fafe abideing can be there.
'Gainft others, or our felves whatever Vice,
We act, are flight and fmall compar'd to this.
Confcious of this, the High Prieft *Eli* faid, *(h)*
If one againft another Sin, remeed
May from the Judge be had; but when the Crime
Is Levell'd at the LORD, who fhall intreat for him?
Who are th' Ungodly here? Some one may cry,
They who the Honour due to GOD deny.
Such are the fools who void of Holy Flame,
Perfwade themfelves that he is but a Name.
Or fuch who do believe a GOD to be,
Yet feign him fuch an one as does not fee,
Or punifh, but who feign him fuch a GOD;

A 2   No.

(e) *Rom:* 1. v: 21. (f) *Rom:* 1. v: 26. (g) *Gen.* 20. v: 11. (h) 1 *Sam:* 2. v: 25.

No God he has, no Truth's in his abode.
And such who to the great Creator say, *(i)*
Depart from us, we don't desire thy way.
What is th' Almighty, that we should obey;
Or where's our profit, if we to him pray ?
But O! how will these Wretches quake for fear,
When this dread Sentence thunders in their ear ;
These Stubborn Rebels who reject my sway, *(k)*
Bring hither quickly, and before me slay.
And such who never lift their hearts to God,
That they may draw a Bliss on their aboad,
Or render thanks for Blessings they have got :
This *David* of th' Ungodly makes a Note. *(l)*
For they whose Hearts no fervent pray'rs affoid,
Nor Trust, nor Fear, Believe, nor Love the Lord.
The name of Men, they don't deserve to wear,
But that of sordid Swine may justly bear :
Who, when the Acorns shake about their Ears,
Eat on, but still no sign of thanks appears.
And they're Ungodly Desperadoes, who
The Honour only due to God bestow
On Creatures, such Lascivious Spend-all Sots,
Who own no other God, but their vile Guts.
And such who say to Gold, thou art my hope,
And think that hoarded Wealth their Life doth prope.

And

(i) Job 21. v: 14, 15. *(k) Luk.* 19. v. 27. *(l) Psal.* 14. v: 4.

And such is he, that maketh Flesh his Arm, (m)
And trusts in Man, to keep him safe from harm ;
Who, knows not, Man no shelter can affoord
To him, whose heart departeth from the Lord.
And such are they, who Creatures place before, (n)
The Great Creator, Blest for ever more.
And such are they, who God some Honour yield,
Yet follow not the way by him reveal'd.
These are the Hypocrites who offer Vows,
And lifeless Worship pay with formal bows,
While yet the Heart's a sleep, nor seek they how (o)
To honour him, as he would have them do.
Not satisfi'd with what he 'th taught them, they
Their own conceits prefer, and those they will obey.
A Form of Godliness, they still retain, (p)
But that the Pow'r thereof they want is plain.
Tho' they profess that they th' Almighty know, (q)
Yet all their Works and Actions tell you no.
Abominable, Disobedient, they
From ev'ry Virtuous Action run astray.
'Tis not the Ship, that's finely painted o'er,
Nor she whose beak's of Argent, or of Or,
But she, who's closly join'd, of solid Wood,
Defy's th' insulting Waves, that's reckon'd good ,
Close to the wind she ly's, her motion swift,

Obeys

(m) Jer: 17. v. 5. (n) Rom. 1. v. 25. (o) Isa. 29. v. 13. (p) 2 Tim: 3. v. 5.
(q) Titus I. v. 16.

No God he has, no Truth's in his abode.
And such who to the great Creator say, *(i)*
Depart from us, we don't defire thy way.
What is th' Almighty, that we fhould obey;
Or where's our profit, if we to him pray ?
But O! how will thefe Wretches quake for fear,
When this dread Sentence thunders in their ear ;
Thefe Stubborn Rebels who reject my fway, *(k)*
Bring hither quickly, and before me flay.
And such who never lift their hearts to God,
That they may draw a Blifs on their aboad,
Or render thanks for Bleffings they have got :
This *David* of th' Ungodly makes a Note. *(l)*
For they whofe Hearts no fervent pray'rs afford,
Nor Truft, nor Fear, Believe, nor Love the Lord.
The name of Men, they don't deferve to wear,
But that of fordid Swine may juftly bear :
Who, when the Acorns fhake about their Ears,
Eat on, but ftill no fign of thanks appears.
And they're Ungodly Defperadoes, who
The Honour only due to God beftow
On Creatures, fuch Lafcivious Spend-all Sots,
Who own no other God, but their vile Guts.
And such who fay to Gold, thou art my hope,
And think that hoarded Wealth their Life doth prope.

And

(*i*) *Job* 21. v: 14, 15. (*k*) *Luk:* 19. v: 27. (*l*) *Pfal.* 14 v: 4

And such is he, that maketh Flesh his Arm, (m)
And trusts in Man, to keep him safe from harm ;
Who, knows not, Man no shelter can affoord
To him, whose heart departeth from the Lord.
And such are they, who Creatures place before, (n)
The Great Creator, Blest for ever more.
And such are they, who God some Honour yield,
Yet follow not the way by him reveal'd.
These are the Hypocrites who offer Vows,
And lifeless Worship pay with formal bows,
While yet the Heart's a sleep, nor seek they how (o)
To honour him, as he would have them do.
Not satisfi'd with what he 'th taught them, they
Their own conceits prefer, and those they will obey.
A Form of Godliness, they still retain, (p)
But that the Pow'r thereof they want is plain.
Tho' they profess that they th' Almighty know, (q)
Yet all their Works and Actions tell you no.
Abominable, Disobedient, they
From ev'ry Virtuous Action run astray.
'Tis not the Ship, that's finely painted o'er,
Nor she whose beak's of Argent, or of Or,
But she, who's closly join'd, of solid Wood,
Defy's th' insulting Waves, that's reckon'd good ;
Close to the wind she ly's, her motion swift,

Obeys

(m) Jer: 17. v. 5. (n) Rom. 1. v: 25. (o) Isa: 29. . 13. (p) 2 Tim: 3. v. 5.
(q) Titus 1. v. 16.

Obeys her rudder, she's the Ship that's right.
External Worships nice performer, who,
With solemn mien to Church doth duely go,
Who never fails the sacred bread to break,
Nor does he e'er the Holy Cup forsake:
Hath but the name of Christ'an yet attain'd,
Unless he by a Holiness unfeign'd,
Attended with a livly Faith adore
Stick closs, and join with Christ his Saviour.
Giant LORD, that we may thee alone adore,
And from our Hearts Ungodliness abhore.
Thou hat'st the Workers of Iniquity, (r)
Thy Curse upon the Wicked's House doth ly (s)
The Wicked's lamp thou'st said shall be put out, (t)
Then who their Miserable State can doubt?
As when unwelcome Night begins its sway,
And throws its sable mantle o'er the Day:
The Traveller a while insults the Night,
And chears himself with Artificial Light;
But when his Night deluding Light's struck blind
A double horror strickes his bodding mind.
Even so,
Th' Ungodly Man may for a Breathing while,
With Worldly wealth his blinded Soul beguile;
But when unthought of Death shall snatch him hence,

He

_____

(r) *Psal.* 5. v. 5. (s) *Prov.* 3. v. 33. (t) *Prov.* 13. v. 9.

He then fhall own the Fond Improvidence.
For when he's Summond hence by Death, he'll leave   (*u*)
All this behind, no Glory's in the grave.
So *David* fay's, the Wicked he had feen   (*x*)
In Pow'r, and like a Bay-tree frefh and green,
Spreading its pleafant Branches all around,
But lo no fign or traft of him he found,
Tho' carefully in every place he fought,
For he was gone, he paft as quick as thought ;
Now fome there are, who hear the Word of GOD,
Communicat, and look like Saints Abroad ;
But, if their inward parts you could furvey,
Hypocrifie alone does all their Actions fway :
Their Voice is *Jacob's*, pleafant, fmooth, and good,
Their hands are *Efau's*, that is full of Blood.
Others put on a Form of Piety,
But ẏet their Hearts with CaresDiftracted be.
Their Money is their GOD, in it they place
Their Truft, their Confidence, and Happinefs.
And from fmall Ventures large acquifts to gain,
Is all the bufie ftudy of their Brain.
In adding heap, to heap is all their care,
They never call on GOD, or very rare.
Others again th' Almighty's Laws reject,
And to their Carnal Wills pay great refpect.

Thefe

(*u*) *Pfal.* 49. v. 17.   (*x*) *Pfal.* 37. v. 35, and 36.

Thefe from their Shoulders fhake CHRIST's eafy Yoak,
And of his Burden light, they make a mock :
They'll rather with the blinded Rabble ftray, (*y*)
And to deftruction run the patent way ;
Then the ftrait Gate and narrow Way purfue,
Which leads to Life, fought after by a few.
Pleafure, the Baud to Vice, firft draws them in ;
Pleas'd with ill Company they're led to fin.
Ill Company, fays *Paul*, corrupts the Good,
He's bleft, in finners ways, who never ftood ; (*z*)
Nor e'er confents, by ill Advice to walk ;
Nor Sits, where Wicked Men profanely talk.
With thofe converfing, who their King adore,
By wicked *Pharoh's* Life, good *Jofeph* fwore.
Thrice in the high Priefts Palace *Peter* li'd,
Thrice he his LORD and Mafter CHRIST deny'd.
No alteration to the better's found.
In fickly perfons who infect the found.
Our Health we can't impart, to give them eafe,
Yet eas'ly we attract their vile Difeafe.
Would you be good, would you be truly Wife,
Then fhun all thofe that take delight in Vice.
Youth haunts with Youth, the Old with Age agree,
Rich Men with Rich have bus'nefs ftill we fee,
Drunkards ftill drunken fots do moft cajole,

And
Our

(*y*) *Matth.* 7. v. 13. and 14. (*z*) *Pfal.* I. v. I.

And Tars with Tars along the Sea Banks roll,
Rabbies of Learned Company make choife,
And ev'ry thing doth in its like rejoice.
In Wife Soci'ties, Wifdom is injoy'd, (a)
But he who haunts with Fools fhall be deftroy'd.
To fuch as fear the LORD, my felf I'll join, (b)
Thofe who their Wills to his Commands refign.
GOD's faving Grace fhould teach us to deny (c)
Ungodlinefs, from Wordly Lufts to fly ;
Should teach us, how we foberly fhould live,
And by our Holy Lives a good Example give.
What loathed Name, then, can their Crime exprefs,
Who turn GOD's Grace into Lafciv'oufnefs.
A Chaft, unfpotted Life, the Heathens faw
Was beft, ev'n fathom'd by the Nat'ral Law.
So *Tully* fpoke, if Mortals would but fcan,(d)
The Dignity, the Excellence of Man;
They foon fhould know,how vile,how much below
Their Nature 'twere, in Luxury to flow :
In Sparing, Chaft, and Sober Honeft Lives,
They'd taft the Sweets, that true Contentment gives.
Tho' without Law, fays *Paul*, by Nature taught, (e)
The things i'th' Law contain'd the Gentiles wrought.
Heav'ns depute Confcience, taught them how to choofe,
Virtue to Praife, and Wickednefs refufe.

B

' They'r

(a) *Prov.* 13. v. 20. (b) *Pfal.* 119 v. 63. (c) *Titus.* 2. v. 12. (d) *Cicero de offic.* (e) *Rom.* 2. v. 14, and 15.

They're Monſters, ſure they don't deſerve the Name
Of Chriſtians, tho they it unjuſtly claim,
Who act thoſe mighty ills, which wiſer Heathens blame.
Ungrateful they, they GOD's free Grace poſtpone,
And in their ſordid luſts ſtill wallow on.
With our firſt Parents thus they go aſtray,
Who taught us firſt to fool our Bliſs away ;
They for an Apple all Mankind betray'd,
Was e'er a more Imprudent bargain made.
With *Eſaus* Folly, theirs may Parallel,
Who, Wretch, devour'd his Birth-Right at a meal.
With *Iſra'ls* madneſs too, theirs may compare,
Who the *Ægyptian* courſe and ſtinking fare
Preferr'd, to all the Bleſſings did attend,
The Wealth ſcarce wiſh'd for of the holy Land.
O what ſtrange Frenzy doth thoſe Men poſſeſs,
Who deem to live in Luſt, a happineſs.
Yet they are worſe, who all the Joys above,
Count nothing when Compar'd with Carnal Love.
But they are Trip'ley mad, who do abuſe
The Goſpel, and by it their vice excuſe,
Or Warrant, who, the Doctrine of free Grace
Pervert, to Patronize their Actions baſe.
So *Paul* long time ago complain'd of ſome, *(f)*
Who ſay'd, let us do ill that good may come :
And that in Wickedneſs we ſhould be found,

That

(f) *Rom:* 3. v: 8.

That fo the Grace of God might more abound.

Peter of thofe Complains who when they fpoke *(g.)*

Great Swelling words, deceiv'd the fimple Fo'k :

Through wantonnefs and luft they Lur'd them in,

And promis'd them a Liberty to Sin.

They did indeed profefs a God to know,

Tho all their works declar'd it was not fo.

So Taught the *Nicolaitans*, and fo *(h)*

The followers of *Simon Magus*, who

So Eagerly Promifcuous Lufts Imbrace,

And Name-them Fruits of Mercy and of *Grace.*

And in thefe latter Days, from this vile Root,

We fee the fame accurfed Tennets Sprout.

Hence Sprung the Wretched *Antinomian* Sect, *(i)*

Who to the Decalogue fhow no Refpect ;

Who Taught, tho Raging *Luft* i'th' Body Reigns,

And tho Intemp'rance burft the Glutted Veins,

Tho Prides Rank Poifon Swells the heaving Breaft,

Or Curs'd Ambition Robs the Soul of Reft,

Tho all the hidden Paths of Sin he Tract,

Which *Devils* know, or Wretched Sinners Act :

If he the Gofpel Promifes believe,

That Juftifies the Wretch, and will him fave.

Of thofe who trufted in this weak belief,

Iftebius accounted was the Chief.

I came the Law and Prophets to fulfill, *(k)*   Not

(g) 2 *Epift.* 2. v: 18, 19. *(h) Irenæus Lib:* 2. *Adverf. Hæres* c: 57. *(i) Sleid Coment Lib:* 12. *Anno* 1538. *(k) Mat.* 5. *v.* 17.

Not to Deſtroy (ſays Chriſt) 'twas ne'er my will.

Do we through Faith make void the Law, ſays *Paul*, *(l)*

The LORD forbid, yea, we eſtabliſh't all.

The Law was not to *Jacob* only ſent, *(m)*

But for a Guide to us 'twas likeways meant.

Nor can I *David George* well here neglect,

The Author of another curſed Sect :

Who boaſted ſome perfection he had found,

Did in himſelf and followers abound,

Which from th' obedience of the Law them free'd,

And taught them in vile Luſt to range with greed.

'Twixt Good and Ill, no dif'rence is at all, *(n)*

'Twixt Life and *Death*, 'twixt riſing and a fall.

Woe unto them who Sirname Evil Good, *(o)*

And what is Good for ill proclaim aloud ·

Who horrid Darkneſs put, for Shinning Light,

Name Light, thick Darkneſs and Eternal night :

Who name that Bitter, which is really Sweet,

What's Bitter, by the Name of Sweetneſs greet.

And next,

My Muſe, the *Romaniſts* 'mongſt them may claſs,

Who turn GOD's Grace into Laſcivioufneſs.

Whilſt Gaudie Pomp and Show, are counted Right,

Theſe Hipocrites internal Worſhip ſlight.

Of Abſtinence, how do they raiſe the price,

Form

(l) Rom. 3. v. 31. *(m)* *Aug. l.b.* 3 *cont.* 2 *Epiſt. Pelag.* *(n) lib.* 3 *Mira. c.* 11. *lit. C. fol.* 13. *Col.* 2. *(o) Iſa.* 5. v. 20.

From certain Meats, who ne'er abſtain from Vice.

This ſort of Hypocrites, you ſee, make clean (p)

The outſide of the Cup, whilſt all within,

Is full of Exceſs, and Extortion ſeen.

All theſe they held accurs'd, and hold them ſtill, (q)

Who ſay, ſince *Adam's* fall there's no Free will.

Sure Prides falſe Light, miſguides the Wandring Mind,

And vain Ambition, ſtrikes the Judgement blind.

So ſaying, Chriſt himſelf, they Curſe, you ſee ;

Who ſays, you can do nothing without me. (r)

Thus *Paul's* Accurs'd, if they may be believ'd,

Who ſays, what have ye that ye han't receiv'd, (s)

That Man's Imagination from his Youth,

Is ill, 's aſſerted by the God of Truth. (t)

O ! would theſe Trumpeters of their own Strength,

And proper Merits, think of this at Length ;

How much ſo e'er, they to themſelves do place,

So much they take away from GODS free Grace.

We ſafer Live by Farr, if we our all

Commit to GOD, than if we neer ſo ſmall

A part, ſhould to our Feeble ſelves Aſcrive,

And Impiouſly encroach on GODS Prerogative.

Their Doctrine Renders heedleſs Men ſecure,

While they Blaſphemouſly the Fools aſſure,

Prieſts Abſolution from all Sin doth free,

Nor

(p) *Matth*. 23. v2 5. (q) *Conc. Trid. Seſſ*. 6. *Can*. 5. (r. *John* 15. v. 5·
(s) 1 *Cor*. 4. v. 7. (t) *Geneſ*. 8. v. 21.

Nor leaves the tincture of Iniquity :
And punishment for Sin they need not fear,
Who pay for Popes Indulgences so dear.
O *Solomon*! had *Rome* been known to thee,
Thou had'st not four, but five things made agree ;
That never say they have enough, one more,
Item, no doubt had been the *Romish* Whore.
Whose heads judge fore reward, whose Priests for hire (*u*)
Do teach, whose Prophets Money doth inspire.
So *Escobar* their Casuist, speaketh plain, (*x*)
No mortal sin it is to Preach for gain :
Or, for vain Glory, tho' your Principal
Design it be, (*y*) ' for all here's set to sale
' Churches, Priests, Altars, Masses, Crowns, and Fire,
' Incense, and Pray'rs ; nay Heav'n and God for~~fire~~ *hire*
' Alas, now Money reigns alone at *Rome*. (*z*)
' Virtue's thence banish'd with an exiles ~~down~~ *down*
What Purgatory makes and keeps ? why Gold
For what but Cash are absolutions sold
For what were Masses, Pilgrimages made,
Dirges, and Pardons ? Gold gain'd by the Trade.

What

(*u*) *Mica* 3. v. 11. (*x*) Additionals to the Mistery of Jesuit. pag. 82.
prop. 29. (*y*) Mantuan poet. lib. calamit. 3.
Venalia nobis
Templa, Sacerdotes, altaria, sacra, coronæ,
Ignis, thura, preces, cœlum est venale, Deusque.
(*z*) *Mantuan Eclog.* 5.
- - - - - - -*Heu* Romæ! *nunc sola pecunia regnat* ;
Exilium virtus patitur.

What is't that makes, and keeps the Nuns and Friers ?

No other Anfwer ftill but Gold appears.

What makes a Card'nal, Bifhop, Prieft, or Pope?

Money's their Maker, ripned mold their Prope:

Heie *Bell* and *Dragon*, *Harpy*, *Maloch*, and

True *Abaddon* and *Appolyon* ftand :

The never fatiat throat devouring all,

Promifcoufly gulps down the great, and fmall.

The gracious fee rejecteth none where Red. (*a*)

Or white, do for the Suppliant interceed.

The *German* Grievances difcover plain, (*b*)

That *Romes* Religion's calculate for gain:

For this alone with Faftings they difpence,

For Gold Unlawful Marriages Licence.

Here Licences (if Luft prevail) for Gold.

Aie, or for Whoreing, or for Inceft fold.

For Murder, Sodomy, or Thift, he may,

Have here a Licence, who can foundly pay.

For Money here the Innocent they curfe,

And them again abfolve for t'other Purfe.

Money abfolves, and *Silver* gives the doom ;   (*c*)

Here ready cafh fills up Repentanc's room.

No Penny, then no *Pater Nofter*, they

Receive no Sacrament, who cannot pay.

Give

(*a*) *Matthew Paris Anno.* 1103. (*b*) *Gravam. Germ. Num.* 1, 2, 3, 4:
&c. (*c*) *Gravam Germ.* 67. 68. *&c.*

Give here devoutly, and to Heav'ns high band *(d)*
' I'll join thee ; for 'tis by the giving hand,
' Sick Souls are wash'd there, People than I say
' Come here, tho' ye live neer so far away ;
' A Rich Reward for ready Cash thou haft,
' Pray Friend make haft ; throw in while yet thou may'ft
' And so forsooth neer doubt of Heaven to tafte.
' Did'ft thou but know, how much thy Gift would grow,
' Thou'dft quickly throw all that thou had'ft to sow.
' I'd have thee wretch, while time is, fly thy pain
' Open thy Purse, that thou may'ft pardon gain.

(d) Cut on an Ancient Stone in the Cathedral Church of
St. *Stephen* at *Bourges ex Chemnit Exam.*. P. 4. C. 4.
S. *de multip. Jubilæor.*

Hic des devote, cœleftibus affocio te :
Mentes ægrotæ per munera funt ibi lota.
Ergo venitote gentes a fede remote ·
Qui datis eftote certi de divite dote.
Te precor accelera, fpargas hic dum potes æra,
Et fic revera fecure cœlica fpèra.
O tu fi fcires, quantum data profit ibi res,
Tu Juxta vires donares quod dare quires.
Te Mifer a pœna dum tempus habes altena,
Ut tibi fit pœna venia, fit aperta crumena.

'Who now gives freely, shall Heav'ns Fabrick see,
'I'm Witness to't, you here may cleansed be.
'Trust me, O trust you shall be plac'd on high
'For your reward, to CHRIST, make room, you'll cry.
'Here paradise is set to sale, then let
'The good Men run, and sease the highest seat.
'Would'st have the market thine? lay down your stock
'Your ready Cash the gates of Heav'n unlock.
'Give largely here, your way to Heav'n is clear,
'Who sparing sows, shall have the meaner chear.
'Why lagg'st thou? but some Money give, alone
'For cash, thou shalt rejoice in Heav'ns high Throne.

Consors cælestis fabrica qui porrigit est is,
Ex hoc sum testis, vos hic mundare potestis.
Crede mihi, crede, cœli donaberis æde;
Nam pro mercede CHRISTO dices, mihi cede.
Hic datur exponi paradisus venditioni;
Currant ergo boni, rapientes culmina throni.
Vis retinere forum? mihi pendas pauca obulorum,
pro summa quorum referabitur aula polorum.
Hic si large des, in cælo fit tua sedes,
Qui serit hic parce, parce comprendit in arce.
Cur tardas? tantum nummi mihi des aliquantum;
Pro solo nummo gaudebis in athere summo.

From

From Ready Cash the Roman Popedome sprung,
By that Encreas'd, by that it stands so long :
Not by true Doctrine, nor severity
Of Discipline, nor Prayer's, nor Sanctity,
Nor by ought els that ever we could hear,
But Readie Cash she did her Fabrick Rear.
My Wonder here is to a Crisis brough't,
That such Good Natur'd things as Popes are thought ;
Do not at once, without one penny Gain,
(No Cash they want, that Pow'r they have is plain)
A Gen'ral Jayle Deliv'ry grant to all,
Who're now in Purgatory, great, and small :
And daily Wipe the Living's Scores away,
That never any more, there enter may.
The rather, since so many of the Souls
In Durance, now, or like to come in Shoals,
Have nor Estates to leave, nor Friends that will,
Or Clear their Debt, or Pay the Jaylors Bill.
I think, the Pope, might twice, or thrice a Week,
Exert his Pow'r, to Liberate the Greek.
And for the Western Church should ev'ry Day,
The Plenitude of's Papal Pow'r Display ;
That so all Christ'ans Dead alreadie, might
Mount strait to Heav'n, and tast Sublime Delight :
And ev'ry one who shall hereafter Die,
Soon as they leave the Earth, to Heaven may Fly :

At

At moft, they only fhould be bound to knock,
At the Black Prifon Door, as 'twere to mock,
And vex the Spitefull Jaylor, to perceive,
How his Revengfull Malice they Deceive.
Soon as they knock, then whoop to Heaven they Fly,
Supported on the Wings of papal Charity.
Either the Pope muft fear, this courfe to take,
Left Heav'n fo full, no room for him could make :
Or which is yet more likely, of the Twain,
In th' other World a Paradife to Gain.
His Papafhip, doth not intend to lofe
The Gain, which Pardons in this World produce.
If fo, I wifh him ferv'd with the fame Sauce,
With which his Commiffar *Tecelius* was.
The Story's this,   *Chemnit.*
A Noble Perfon to this Fellow comes,
As he was gath'ring in Prodigious Summs,
From Fools, who Frankly gave what Induftry,
And Toil procur'd, for Pardon Pedlery.
And tells him, in his Lab'ring mind, he had
A Strange and black Atchievment very bad.
A Patent for this Future Crime he wants,
Or Pardon which you pleafe, the Pedler grants
His wifh, but tells him fuch Commiffions were
(Moft Reafonable fure) fold very Dear :
To Chaffering they come, and fo at laft,

A Bargain's *Struck*, the readie Cafh in haft;
The Merchant pay's down on the nail, and takes.
His Bull, then ftrait to fome near Wood he makes·
Not long perdue the watchfull *Robber* lay,
Conceal'd, e'er he perceiv'd his pedling Prey
A Trav'ling, Stor'd with wares and readie Money,
And Robs my Chap-man there of ev'ry Penny.
The Pardon-pedler, Brandifh'd ftrait a whole
Shop-full of Curfes, at the Robbers Soul :
Who fhow'd his High-pric'd Bull, and laughing faid,
This was the Sin I meant, for this I Pay'd.
The Simple Goofe So's by the Arrow fhot,
Wing'd by the Feathers which from him it got.
But what I Pray, have we to do with Man, (*a*)
That his Confeffion, we fhould hear or Scan ?
As if a Man could Cure a Wounded mind,
Or, for our Sins now paft, a Salve could find ;
A Curious pack, to know anothers ill,
Whilft to ammend themfelves they fhow no will.
Who can a Sinfull Soul fiom Hell Reprieve, (*b*)
Or who but GOD alone can Sins Forgive.
Who think by Money, that they may acquire,
Eternal Life, and Scape Eternal Fire ;
What *Peter* faid to *Magus* let them hear.
Thy Money perifh with thee 'caufe thou'ft thought, (*c*)

The

(*a*) *Aug. lib.* 10. *confeff. c.* 3.　(*b*) *Marc.* 2 v: 7.　(*c*) *Acts.* 8. v: 20 & 21

The Gift of Heav'n with Money might be bought.
Thou in this matter haft nor part, nor lot,
Right in the fight of God thy heart is not.
Next wee the Character of *Rome* fhall fee,
With that of thofe Seducers doth agree ; (d)
Who in the latter days fhould come and teach,
The felf fame Doctrine which the Devils Preach.
Forbidding Marriage, to their Priefts and Monks,
Tho' ev'ry Cloifter fwarms with Rogues and Punks.
The Pope himfelf's the Baud, that draws them in,
And fhows his bald-pate crew the way to fin.
He like a cunning Pandar reaps the gains,
Whilft the poor Lab'ring Whore takes all the pains.
For more than Twenty Thoufand Duckats, he,(e)
Makes yearly of thefe Whores Iniquity.
But hold, fays one, you tell his Hol'nefs fees,
And how he doth the Wantons Pocket fqueez.
But you neglect the fumpt'ous Houfes, he
Provides; for thofe grown old in Letchery :
His gratitude you fhould not thus pafs o'er,
Who fo maintains the forlorn hoary Whore.
I beg your pardon Sir, and do agree
With what you fay ; of all whores *Romes* muft be
The happ'eft, and of all the Bauds the top,
The gen'roufeft, the kindeft is the Pope.

Rapes,

_____

(d) 1 *Tim.* 4. v. 1. & 3. (e) *Agrip. de van. fcient. Cap.* 64.

Rapes, Incests, Murders, and Adultery,
All these amongst his shavelings I see,
These are their sports, these their diversions be.
Witness that Poem Prelate *Cassa* wrot, (f)
And Printed it, least it should be forgot;
Julius the third's the subject of his lays,
How does he cull his words, his Sodomy to Praise:
Names it a divine help, and owns that he
Nor lov'd, nor us'd another venerie.
What Lusts in Nun'ries Reign, I need not name,
Their Murd'red Infants scarce conceal their shame.
Well may we call Monks Fathers for their breed
Is stock enough to People Earth for need.
What Nations have their Oaths, and Vows betray'd,
Which vanish in the breath, with which they're made.
What need I any more Examples bring,
Than the sad story of th' *Ungarian* King.
Uladislaus, what dool, what dismal work,
Follow'd his breach of Faith, with *Amurath* the *Turk*?
The valiant King, most of his Noble Train,
And treach'rous (g) *Julian*, in the Battle slain.
He's blest who to his Vows hath firmly stood, (h)
Who promiseth to's loss, yet makes that promise good.
Saul's Fam'ly was destroy'd, to expiat, (i)
The Cov'nant with the *Hivites* violat.

Rouse

(f) Sleid *Anno* 1550 (g) *Cardinal* Julian *sent by* Pope Eugene *the fourth,
to persuade* Uladislaws, *to break Peace with the* Turk, *slain by the Christians in his
flight, as the Author of their Misfortune.* (h) *Psal.* 15. v. 4. (i) 2 *Samuel* 21.

Roufe yee, yee Kings, fhake off th' ufurping Whore,
VVhilft fhe endures, your Crowns are not fecure.
VVhat Subjects hath fhe forc'd to difobey?
VVhat Crowns, and Kingdoms doth fhe gift away ?
Attabaliba King of *Peru*, thou
This to thy Tragical experience knew :
Thou wifely might'ft, and did'ft conclude, the *Pope*,
Either to be fome noble crazy fop ;
VVho what was not his own fo frankly gave,
To ev'ry fycophantick gapeing flave :
Or, fure his impudence muft needs be great,
His unjuft knav'ry of the foremoft rate,
VVho thy Poffeffions thus did give away,
And armed Strangers fent, thy Subjects for to flay.
Nor was his Tyranny alone confin'd,
To th' unknown VVorld, thou *England* too did'ft find
Th' effects o't, when thou from thy chalky Shoars,
Perceiv'dft the *Spanifh* Fleet advance with Sails and Oars :
Tho' Heav'n was kind, and made th' Invaders graves,
I'th' breakings of fome tenth, unlucky waves.
How may thofe Artifts of their skill repent,
VVho perifh by the Arts they do invent.
Nor did they, thy *Elizabeth*, effay,
Only by open VVars to take away,
No, *Ballard*, *Campian*, *Perfons* all the fry
Of curfed Antichriftian fools, did try,

By

By private ſtabbing, to be cannoniz'd;
Tho' e're they wrought the ill, they were ſurpriſ'd,
And felt deſerved pain, for being, ſo ill adviſ'd.
Nor can the free-born *Brittains* have forgot,
The Antichriſtian Helliſh Powder Plot.
Thou *France*, who now ſo ſoundly ſeem'ſt to ſleep,
And giv'ſt the treacherous Wolf thy Sheep to keep,
Haſt thou forgot (*k*) his Holineſs, who will'd
That *Monk*, a Saint, who thy third *Henry* kill'd.
And thy fourth *Henry* too, by Rav'llac ſlain,
Who thought by Murd'ring Kings, a place in Heav'n to (gain.
Thou mind'ſt (*O Delph*) for ſure, you ha'n't forgot
The treach'rous *Gerhaurd*, who thy Darling ſhot;
William, the firſt of *Orange*, bold in Fight,
Who could to Action thy faint Troops excite;
None better underſtood the Art of War,
None more the Souldiers, or Commanders care,
Thou weſtern Cæſar too, art in the lurch, (*l*)
According to the cuſtoms of the Church:
When e'er his Holineſs intends to hunt,
'Tis thou muſt hold the ſtirrop, till he mount:
Or if he viſiteth ſome holy Corſe,
Thou by the Bridle, lead'ſt the prancing Horſe.
Or does his Holineſs intend to eat, (*m*)
(For Earthly GODS ſubſiſt not without Meat)

The

(*k*) *Sixtus* 5. (*l*) *Ceremon. Rom. Ecc. lib.* 1. *Sect.* 5. *pag.* 4. *fol.* 61. (a. b.)
(*m*) *Ceremon. Rom. Ecc. lib.* 1. *Sect.* 3. *Pag.* 1. *fol.* 43. (b)

The *Semper Auguft* with the bafon ftands,
'Till *Holinefs* thinks fit to wafh its hands:
No Monarch ever had a piettier Poft,
Betwixt the Stable and the Bafon toft.
For thy bafe flav'ry, thou'rt alone to blame,
And lefs to be bewail'd with Tears, than fhame.
Who makes God's Law his buf'nefs, and delight, (*n*)
Who meditates therein, by Day, and Night,
Is Bleft, fays *David*; but, the Pop'lings fay,
He's curft who reads therein by Night or Day.
And why crys one? the Reafon Sir is plain,
Where e're the Sciiptur's read, their Dagon's flain.
But, haik, a bulky Prieft bauls out aloud,
We have a vulgar Bible, Sir, as good
As any extant, nay, if Church may be
Believ'd, alone is of Authoritie.
Peiufe that Bible, Sir, therein you'll find, (*o*)
So many *Barbarifms* are contain'd,
So many *Solæcifms*, that I fear,
Did fuch in School-Boys exercife appear,
(Suppofe him Popifh) would the labour fave,
Of Pennance voluntar, to little knave.
Here are Additions to the Woid, and there,
Subtractions from th' Authentick Text appear.
This verfe is alter'd to a diff'rent fenfe,

D

And

(*n*) *Pfal.* i. v. 2. (*o*) *Apud Petrum Santandreanum*, Anno 1614.

And that a plain contrary does difpence ;
But thefe I pafs, I'll only let you hear,
Some famples of flat nonfenfe that appear.
As for Example.

In Peace into that thing, I'll fleep and reft. (p)
When e'er a Chappel's to our bedlam made,
This Text, that's here, fo wittily expreft,
Be Preach'd on by a Fry'r, to make the People glade.

And in the Night I'll cry, and not to me, (q)
To Foolifhnefs. E'en let this handled be
Bv fome good *Jefuite* in the forefaid place
In th' Afternoon he'll do it with a Grace.

I am converted, in my Miferie, (r)
Whil'ft is thruft in a thorn, and let this be
Thought on by fome wife Penitentiarie.

My Loins are with illufions fill'd. This fmells (s)
Full rankly of the Cloifter Droning-bees,
Where if wee may believe, what ftory tells,
Both Brains, and Loyns, are fick o'th' fame Difeafe.
None but a Schoolman, furely this fhould fing. (t)

Of

(p) *Pfal.* 4. v. 8. *in pace in id ipfum, dormiam & requiefcam.* (q) *Pfal*
21. v. 2. with them, Ours *Pfal* 22. v. 2. latter part, *& nocte clamabo, &*
non ad infipientiam mihi. (r) *Pfal.* 31. v. 4. Ours *Pfal.* 32. v. 4. *Converfus*
fum in arumna mea, dum configitur fpina. (s) *Pfal.* 37. v. 7. Ours *Pfal.*
38. v. 7. *Lumbi mei impleti funt illufionibus.* (t) *Pfal.* 67 v. 13. and 14. Ours
Pfal. 68. v. 12. and 13. *Rex virtutum dilecti dilecti. & fpeciei domus divide-*
re fpolia Si dormiatis inter medios cleros, penna columba de argentata, &
pofteriora dorfi ejus in pallore auri.

Of the Belov'd, of the Belov'd the King.
Of Virtues, and for to divide the spoils,
Of Beauty of the House (the sense recoils)
If in the middle of the Clergy ye
Sleep, Pigeons Wing sure *guilt with Silver be,*
And the posteriors of his back behold,
Are in the paleness of the Ev'ry Gold.
Our years shall as the Spider meditate, (*u*)
(Note here ! the Spider's a most studious brat.)
Now, *in themselves our Years, are threescore ten,*
Or seventy Years, as from this Text is plain ;
But if wee're in Dominion eighty Years
(Here the desir'd Catholicon appears,
All ye that would live long, take care to be
Thrust into places of Authoritie.
Hereafter Labour is of them and grief
Because that meekness comes, just like a Thief,
That's, *unexpectedly, and wee'll be ta'en*
Full suddenly, O ! for a cunning Man,
Or Tom-a-bedlame, to pick sense out off,
This conj'ring if you please or canting stuff.
These for a swatch of Nonsense, next you'll find
Good Works is all their cry, yet oh ! how blind
Are they, what darkness hath o'er spread their mind. }

(*u*) *Psal.* 89. v. 10, 11, 12. Ours *Psal.* 90. v. 9. & 10. *Anni nostri sicut aranea meditabuntur : dies annorum nostrorum in ipsis, septuaginta anni : Si autem in potentatibus, octoginta anni & amplius eorum labor & dolor. Quoniam supervenit mansuetudo, & corripimur.*

What one, of all the Precepts ten, do they
Not plainly contradict, and difobey.
No other Gods before me, thou fhalt have, (x)
Thus fpoke the Lord, but fee the Papal knave
Hath *Mary*, *Peter*, *Paul*, and Thoufands more,
Whom they before the only God adore.
Thou fhalt not make an Image of the Lord, (y)
Nor fhall the Creatur's likenefs be ador'd.
Thus fpeaks the Law ; but on the contrair, they
To fenfelefs Statues Adoration pay :
Wax Candles light, and fet before the ftock,
Churches and Chappels build, where they Invock
The ftump, nor do they mifs to fet apart
A Holy Day to tickle't to the heart.
Through dirt, and mire, barefoot, the fenfelefs rout
Hoble along, to find his Godfhip out ;
And doing fo, conclude themfelves devout.
The old Seducer ftrove ; but ftrove in vain,
The prudent *Mofes*'s Body to obtain :
Th' Arch-angel him withftood, the *Jews* he knew,
The Body once obtain'd, would worfhip't too:
But mark, what here he mifs'd, at *Rome* he gain'd,
No fooner he attempt'd, but he obtain'd,
The Bodies of the Saints-fhould be ador'd,
And all the Churches with their reliques ftor'd.

In

(x) 1 Command. (y) 2 Command.

In ev'ry Church, Arms, Fingers, Foot, or Hand,
Afhes, and Cloaths, for Adoration ftand.
That in *Rome* Chrift'an, Satan this hath gain'd,
Is clearly in the *Trentin* Acts contain'd. (z)
Thus they command, the Martyr's Bodies fhou'd
Be worfhipt, and order'd by all the crowd;
For doing fo, will benefits draw down,
And the Adorers Life, with Bleffings Crown.
All thofe they Damn, who fay no Honour's due,
Or Worfhip to the Saints: they vainly fue
For help to them, in vain they haunt their fhrines
Who neither know, nor further, their defigns.
They teach the Reliques of the Saints deceaf't, (a)
Are with a Supernat'ial pow'r poffeft;
That healeth Maladies, Infernal Pow'rs
Drives out, and fanctifies both us and and ours.
A Fire in *Cologne*, great deftruction made, (b)
The Flames, the Church it felf, dar'd to invade:
'Till the (c) Arch-Prelate, *Cunberts* Body brought
Before the Fire, and his Protection fought:
Scarce had he fpoke, when ftraight the Flames obey,
Fly from the Corfe, fhrink back and faint away.
The gazing Crowd, who faw the hafty flight,
Conclude his Merits great, as well they might.
To Relicts, Afhes, nay to very Cloaths,

They

(z) *Sef.* 24. (a) *Tho Aquin. fecunda fecunda queft.* 96. *Art.* 4: (b) *Au*
thor Sacrarii urbis colon. pag. 60. (c) *Sigewin.*

They pay their Vows, by them they ſwear their Oaths.

There is a piece of Linnen, mark the tale,

Which they have chriſt'ned *Holy Vernacle*,

Our SAVIOUR, at His Paſſion, as they ſay,

With it, did wipe, from's Face, the ſweet away;

But as he wip'd, a lively Picture of

His Face, remain'd imprinted on the ſtuff.

This precious Relict to this very day

They keep, and to it this *Orizon* ſay.

' Hail Holy Face of our Redeemer, in *(d)*

' Which beauty of Divineſt Grace doth ſhine;

' Imprinted on a Snow white Cloth by GOD,

'Loves pledge, upon the Vernacle beſtow'd.

' We pray thee, be a buckler, and relief

' To us, a ſweet refreſhment, from our grief

' Comfort us; that our Foes may never hurt

' Us, but we may within thy Heav'nly Court

' Injoy a bleſſed Reſt for ay with thee

             Amen

(d) Horæ Beat. Virg. ad Rit. Eccl. Sariſb. fol. 74. Pariſ 1534.

Salve ſanctâ facies noſtri redemptoris,

In qua nitet ſpecies divini ſplendoris,

Impreſſa panniculo nivei candoris,

Dataque Veronicæ ſignum ob amoris.

Eſto nobis, quæſumus, ſcutum & Juvamen,

Dulce refrigerium, atque conſolamen;

Ut nobis non noceat hoſtium gravamen;

Sed fruamur requie cœli tecum, Amen.

' *Amen*, O Holy Face fo may it be.

How may'ft thou *Rome* of thy Religion brag ?

Who pay'ft fuch ftrange Devotions to a rag.

They teach the Bodies of the long deceaf'd,

Should from the filent grave be mov'd, and plac'd

Beneath the Altar, where a Box of Gold,

Or Silver, doth the faintlings Body hold.

Here *Dunces* Divine Adoration pay,

And fillily throw all their Wealth away.

See how the giddy crowd prefs, to adore

The cafe, that holds the Bones of rampant whore,

Or Murderer perchance, for furely, they

Saints Relicts are not all, to which they Pray.

The *Virgin Mary*'s Milk fo much encreaft,

No Town fo fmall, where it you might not tafte ;

No Nun'rie, Monaftrie, or Abbey, fo

Obfcure, which could not plenty of it fhow.

So much there was, that tho' her breafts had been   *(e)*

Larger, than thofe the beft Milch Cows are feen

To wear, nay had her Life been fol'ly fpent

In Nurfing, yet her Milk could ne'er augment

To fuch a quantity, as Pop'lings fhew,

At ev'ry place, to the unthinking crew.

A King there was, nam'd *Gerion* once in *Spain*,

Three Heads he had, no lefs as Poets feign.

How

(e) Calvin. admonitio de reliq. Geneva 1597. *p.* 282.

How would it help thofe Relict-wrights, could they
But, as much for their *John* the Baptift fay.
'Tis faid, that *Herodias* Daughter got
The head, and very likely is it not,
That this Wretch, or her Mother, *Herods* Whore,
Should keep it for a Relict to adore?
And yet the People of St. *Ang'lick* fay, (*f*)
They have his Face unto this very day.
Hold there the Town of *Amiens* cry, give place,
For wee alone can fhow the *Baptift's* Face.
Malta the reft o'f's head pretends to keep,
Tho' once at *Rhodes*, it quietly did fleep.
Nemours cry loud they have the hinder part,
And *Novium* keeps the Brains, as they affert.
St. *John Morienni* part of it retains,
A Jaw-bone too at *Befanfon* remains.
Another part's at *Paris*, and the tip
Of's Ear, *St. Flowers* full carefully doth keep.
His Heir and Forehead, trav'led into *Spain*.
Noyon a bit has, and yet once again
Luca has part, tho' all befides his Face.
Wee fhow'd juft now, did *Rhodes*, or *Malta grace*.
But, that's a trifle, do but go to *Rome*,
No fooner you to St. *Silvefters* come,
Than you may fee the head, whole and intire,

Or

Or elſe the Keeper's a notor'ous Lyar.

Next, for the Croſs, and Nails, the Nails were three,

As *(g) Socrates*, and *(h) Ruffin* do agree.

Helena found them, and as ſhe thought beſt,

Half of the Croſs, ſhe laid up in a Cheſt

At *Salem*, t'other half to *Rome* ſhe ſent,

To her Imperial Son a Complement.

One of the Nails was on his Bridle worn,

The other two his Helmet did adorn.

Simon thy Bones were Braſs, thy Sinews ſteel, *(i)*

Who did'ſt not under ſuch a burden reel.

There's ſo much extant of this Holy Wood, *(k)*

As might a Third Rate Ship intirely load.

And for the Nails, unleſs the Prieſts us cozen,

The three are grown a good round Bakers dozen.

Millain, the Bridle Nail claims as its own,

Carpentras ſays with them, 'tis to be ſhown.

Rome has a third and fourth, St. *Helens* and

St. *Croſſes* Churches, theſe two Nails Command.

At *Sien* one, at *Venice* one we ſee,

I think that's pretty fair for *Italy*.

Germany hath her ſhare, at *Colen* is

The ſeventh, aſleep the eight at *Tryers* ly's.

France muſt not loſe its due, at *Paris* in

The *Holy Chappel*, one is to be ſeen.

E   The

(g) *Socr.at. hiſt. lib. 1. c. 13.*(h)*Ruff. hiſt. lib. 1. C. 8.* (i) *Mark c. 15. v. 21.*
(k) *Eraſmus Navis onerariæ juſtum onus.*

The *Carmelites* there likeways keep the Tent,
Th' eleventh I think was to *St. Dennis* lent.
Bowrges the twelft retains, and it appears,
The thirteenth's at the Abbey call'd the *Sheeres.*
The fourteen's at *Draguinian,* hence wee see
How ftrangely Romifh Relicks multiply.
GOD's Holy Name in vain, thou fhalt not take, (*l*)
So fays the Law, but fee the Popl'ings make
Their Solemn Oaths of no effe&, whilft they,   .
No Faith is to be keept with Her'ticks fay :
By dubious and equivocating Speech,
That is by Lies and Perjury, they teach
Their wife Heads may the Hereticks deceive,
For doing this they have the Churches leave.
Remember, let it not flip from your mind, (*m*)
To keep the Sabbath Holy as defign'd.
Thus fpeaks the Law, thefe would-be-Clergy fay,
There's more refpe& due to a Saintlings Day.
And when on Sabbath Days the Prieft appears,
He with Romantick ftuff, treats his Auditors Ears .
Or elfe fome fenfelefs Ceremonies he
Makes ufe of, to atra& th' admiring Eye.
Around the Temple, Crofs and *Banner* walk,
And fometimes with the long deceas'd he'll talk.
Wax Candles muft be lighted, pray you mark,

The

The *Dead* abhore converfing in the dark.
Before fome Image, fpite of the Command,
See he and's fenfelefs croud kneel, ftoop and ftand.
Who finfully thus pafs the time away,
Can ne'er be faid to fanctify the Day.
Honour thy Parents, fee thou them obey, (*n*)
Thus fpeaks the Law, not fo the Pap'lings fay,
The Cloifter ent'red once, the Mortals be
Fiom all obedience to their Parents free;
In teaching fo, they with the *Pharifees* agree. (*o*)
Seeft thou thy forlorn Parents ftarving ly,
Whil'ft thou, who can'ft relieve them, lets them die.
Seeft thou thy Brother begging for his Bread,
Or thy young Sifter perifhing for need:
Tho' their laft breath is ready to expire,
And they muft next to Deaths dark cell retire:
Relieve them not, but leave thy Wealth to me,
Thus fays that would-be Church, and I'll fromHell you free.
Thou fhalt not Kill, fo fays the Holy Law. (*p*)
Their Priefts thus teach, let no bafe fear o'er awe
Your Minds, no, like unthinking *Heroes* kill,
Who e'er refifts the *Popes* Tyrannick Will.
If you efcape, to you wee'll Trophies raife; (*q*)
Our never dying Verfe fhall eternize your Praife:
If otherways, it fhall be faid, here lyes

E 2
` To

To God, and Men, a grateful Sacrifice.

She who her Father, now with Age grown gray, (r)

Did in the *Paris* Maſſacre betray ;

Her Father Dead, the *Parricide* did wed,

Was in this curſed Doctrine Learn'dly Read.

Man's rage they fear, when they would act a ſin,

But dread not Heav'n, nor the great Judge within.

With brutiſh rage to blackeſt ills they run,

And ſcarſcely fear the wickedneſs when done.

The Law Commands, from all Uncleanneſs, wee (s)

Should keep our ſelves, unſpotted, clean and free.

They teach, the Prieſt whoMarries ſinneth more, (t)

Then he who keeps a Concubine or Whore.

The Law Commands us, that we ſhould not Steal. (u)

But theſe Diſturbers of the Common-weal,

Prepare them, like a crew of ſturdy Thieves,

To Rob him, who the Goſpel Truths believes.

By theſe *Banditi* ſpoil'd the helpleſs Prey,

Wounded and rob'd, are left upon the way :

Or baniſht, fly their Native Country, while

The Rogues divide among themſelves, the ſpoil.

Falſe Teſtimony 'gainſt thy Neighbour, thou (x)

ſhalt not adduce, nor back it with a Vow.

Thus ſpoke the Law, but you may quickly ſee,

Their practiſe doth not with this Law agree.

What

(r) *Martyrol. majus edit. Germ. pag.* 1618. (s) 7 *Command.* (t) *Coſterus in Ench. Tract. de Cælebatu.* (u) 8 *Command.* (x) 9 *Command.*

What lyes, what Calumnies, do they not ufe
To Governours, and Princes, to Traduce
The unfeign'd Worfhippers of CHRIST, while they
Take all for granted, that the Pop'lings fay.
The Magiftrat's a Bigot, then the Charge
Is, they'll o'erturn the Churches Sacred Barge:
They're Hereticks, they're Sacrilegious, they
Steal from the Church, the Golden GODS away.
Or is the Prince to *Tyrrany* inclin'd,
The fureft way to ftrike his Fearfull mind,
Is to Allarm him with Sedition's noife,
And baul out Treafon, with a Trumpet Voice.
Or, if the Magiftrate profefs to be
A Man of moralls, and Integrity,
Then the Loud Cry muft be, they're Foes to all
That Men or Honefty, or modeft call.
What e'er's thy Neighbours thou fhalt not defire,(*y*)
From it abftain, for fo the Laws Require.
Their Champions, Evill Concupifcence, fay, (*z*)
To Sin Orig'nal, does not any way
Pertain, nor is it felf a Sin, nor do
They give't its proper Name, who Term it fo.

Two Sacraments our LORD Ordain'd, no more,
The *Romanifts* add five more to that Score:

And

(*y*) 10 *Command.* (*z*) *Bellarm. lib.* 5. *de amiff. grat. & ftat. pecc. cap.* 5.

And as they order matters, to their shame
There's hardly one of CHRISTs now left with them.
The Filching wasp, the Butcher doth not Love,
The Flesh-flys still less welcome to him prove.
That takes away, yet leaves the Fleshes sound,
But what this adds, makes Rotteness abound.
Six Hundred years are Scarcely past, since they
Began this Trade, till *Peter Lombards* Day
Their Shops were shut. But when a deep mouth'd Hound
Opens, the eagre pack the Echo Sound.
So tho before his Day the count was even,
E'er since, the World doth Ring with Number seven
And was it not most Wonderfull, that he
So Earlie made this Rare Discoverie.
There's Holy orders first, we first it Name,
'Cause for their Lot, the Clergy it do claim.
The Laity crave one too for their *Share*,
Nam'd Matrimonie. and their tender Care
For Christ'ans young, a third one doth produce,
'Tis Confirmation, only for their use.
Pennance, to Lapsed Christians alone
Pertains, and those whom Sickness Hurrys on,
A last Anointing, makes them Nimbler run.
I think, I need not Name the other two,
Their Names and uses, ev'ry Christ'an know.
The five I Nam'd are so, so very late,

They need no other Anſwer, than their Date.
Nor Text, nor Author old, nor reaſon found,
For their Support, beyond that *Æra's* found.
Now Baptiſme and the *Euchariſt*, we ſee
Do with the Holy Word of GOD agree,
As Proteſtants receive and uſe them, but
The Shavelings make them a meer Beggars Coat :
So many naſty Patches, on them are,
Scarce one inch of the firſt Stuff doth appear.
Should I but Name what they aſcribe unto
Their Sacraments, that for a proof might go.
Grace in themſelves, the Sacraments contain. *(a)*
(Juſt as the Pots, the Medicines retain.)
That Grace they always give, they think is right
(Ev'n as the Fire gives heat, or Sun gives Light.)'
They upon ev'ry Soul this Grace Diſtill,
(Or Good, or bad, no matter all the while.)
Plain's the command of JESUS CHRIST we ſee,
That in the Name o'th' Bleſſed Trinitie,
His Miniſters with Water ſhould Baptize,
But this, it ſeems, did not the Pop'lings pleaſe. *(b)*
Prieſt, Layman, Male, or Female, Chriſt'an, nay
A *Jew*, or *Turk*, may do't as well they ſay.
How do they from our SAVIOUR's precept ſwerve,
No leſs than two and Twenty patches ſerve

Their

(*a*) *Concil Trid. Seſſ.* 7. *c.* 6. 7. 8. (*b*) *Bell. de eff. Sacr, li.* 2. *c.* 1. 9.

Their Chriftning to Adorn, tho by mifhap, (c)
One has (the more's the lofs) made its Efcape :
Still Twenty one, a jolly crew remain,
Enough to make an honeft Man maintain,
No Ordinance of CHRIST it is;   But you
Would hear them Nam'd, yes Sir I fhall a few
Cull out to fave your Longing, and the reft,
From what is Nam'd, may eafily be gueft.
Firft then the *Prieft*, the *Devil* to be fure
Out of the Partie, fails not to Conjure.
This Charm muft not conclude the common way,
Through CHRIST our LORD, that Satan wont obey ;
But if he fay, *Through him that is to Judge*
The World by Fire, the *Devil* muft not Grudge.
The Reafon from the Cardinal appears,
Old Nick the Day of Judgement chiefly fears.
Another Exfufflation is defign'd,
That is a puffing hard, the more the Wind,
The fooner he'll the Evil Spirit Rout,
And Good Jumps in, when e'er the ill comes out.
A Third is putting holy Salt in's Mouth,
Perhaps you'll think this is to raife his Drouth,
Oh no ! this kills the Worms of Sin, and keeps
The Soul from Putrefaction, when it Sleeps :
Or els perhaps its giv'n as 'tis moft juft,

To

(c) *Bell. de Baptifm. l. 1. c.* 25. 26. 27.

To give the following Fulsom dish a Gust.
Next on his Nose and Ears, some Spittle's laid,
And when the word *Epheta* once is said,
Oh! how it fits his Senses, to receive
All Sp'iritual Objects, by the Fathers leave.
But firstly, he's Anointed on the Crown
With Holy Crism, which certainly is known
By Bishop to be made, and reason Good,
The Bishop is not always understood
To be at hand, and this does well the while.
For if a Man cannot his Belly fill,
A bit to stay the Stomach sure is Good,
Till he can get a larger share of Food.
A Lighted Taper's put into his hand,
To make th' Admiring Gossips understand,
That from Thick Darkness and Substantial Night,
The Baptiz'd is Translated into Light.
The purity of's Soul, next to denote,
They put on's back a fair white Linnen Coat.
Now these I think may serve you for a taste,
And Teach you how to Judge of all the rest:
Were they practis'd with all their pageantry
In Her'ticks view, (as they us dignify)
Sure all the merry grigs would there resort,
No Puppet-show could make a better sport.
But mark, th' effects will make your wonder stretch, (*a*)

F

Not

(*d*) *Concil. Trid. Sess. 5. Decr. 5. Bell. de Baptism. l. 1. c. 13.*

Not only by their Chriftning (as they teach)
Is all Sin fo remov'd, as not to be
Imputed, but as Council doth decree,
It leaves no Sin Inherent, nought remains
As Sin to be Imputed, or that Stains.
Hence you may guefs, who's Baptiz'd by a Prieft,
Muft needs be Sinlefs for a while at leaft.
So *Paul*, and *James*, and *John* (who did not doubt
To fay that Sin in all abides) are plainly out.
Next the neceffity, they on it lay, (*e*)
Is odd, for as the Cardinall doth fay,
The Church always beleiv'd that Infant loft,
Who, e'er it was Baptiz'd, gave up the Ghoft.
And hereupon they found the Liberty
For any to Baptize, as you above may fee.
Their Chrift'ning of Church Bells I fhall but name, (*f*)
Of which ev'n *Bellarmine* himfelf thought fhame.

Now for the *Eucharift*, yet we have feen
But Scratching of the Finger with a pin ;
But here's prefented on the other part,
Deep Stabbings with a Dagger at the Heart.
This is the greateft pledge of JESUS Love,
And hence it doth the chiefeft object prove
Of Satans Spite, which makes his Eldeft Son
His Art out-do, to muddifie this one.

They

(*e*) *Bell. de Baptifm. l. 1. c. 4. Semper Ecclefia credidit infantes perire fi abfque Baptifmo de hac vita recedant.* (*f*) *de Rom. pap. l. 4. c. 12.*

They wed the Fountain to the Gen'rous vine, (g)

And mixing Water Spoil the Fragrant Wine.

The Prieſt Drinks all the Wine himſelf, and truely

Were it not daſh'd, it might prove too unruly.

Sure they, where no Wine grows, break no Commands,

'Tis daſh'd enough alreadie to their hands.

Next, we ſhall ſee how they the Bread abuſe,

None other but Unleav'ned here they uſe :

A Fooliſh Superſtition, where was't ſaid,

Our SAVIOUR any ſuch Reſtriction laid,

As not to uſe what Bread was common, there,

Where the Communicants at preſent were.

For Leav'ned Bread the *Grecian-Church* contends,

Unleav'ned Cakes the *Latine-Church* defends :

And yet a Prieſt his Office loſt ; becauſe

His Bread was Leav'ned, Wine unmixed was.

For Sp'ritual Food a Wafer Cake they chooſe,

What Country, City, Town, can they produce

Where Men for Bread ſuch Tiny-cruſtlings uſe.

Yes Crys Sir *Thomas*, (h) There's a Country fam'd,

I Chriſtned it, I it *Utopia* Nam'd,

In Engliſh, *no Place*, where the Natives Good,

No People Nam'd, make it their daily Food :

No wonder then no Chriſt'ans (but the Name)

Make ſuch a mighty Buſtle for the ſame.

F 2

But

(g) *Non poſſit ſine gravi peccato omitti Bel. de Euch. l. 4. C. 10.* (h) Sir
Thomas More.

But if you would the unknown Mift'rie fift,
Here Tranfubftantiation gets a lift:
For if it be no Bread, it may with eafe
Be fomewhat els, that's Flefh Sir if you pleafe.
Of thefe, there only muft be broken, one,
In Pieces three, eat by the Prieft alone :
As for the Laicks they muft have it whole,
A broken Cake wou'd damn a Lay-mans Soul.
Quite without Book, the former fancy was,
And this is plain againft the Holy Laws.
Our SAVIOUR CHRIST took Bread and it did break,
Of it did all his Difciples partake :
And fhall their Impudence efcape who twit,
Our SAVIOURS practife with the want of wit
For as the Priefts is o'er the Chalice broke,
Left any particle of it fall by,
Intire 'tis given to the Laick Fo'k,
T'avoid Forfooth that very Jeopardy.
To Confecration next we fhall proceed,
Which lies precifely in thefe words we Read, (1)
Thus is my Body, This my Blood. Indeed,
Our Bleffed LORD and SAVIOUR as we Read,
Firft took, next Bleff'd, and then he broke the Bread.
Then to his Difciples he gave't, and made
Them Eat, and laft *This is my Body* faid.

Now

Now here we fee 'twas Bleft, before 'twas broke,

E'er he thefe words *This is my Body* fpoke.

The Prieft muft fpeak the words, but left the Flock *(k)*

Them hear, they're Whifper'd, is not this a mock,

That Publick Acts of Solemn Worfhip fhou'd,

Be done fo privately, that they're not underftood.

But hear the ills from fpeaking loud that flow,

And Weighty Reafons giv'n for fpeaking low.

Fir ft *Hanahs* Voice unheard was, tho the lip *(l)*

Did move, and fhe was of the Church a Type.

But next the Prieft might mar his own defire,

And then the Fat would all be in the Fire.

Thirdly his Voice might fail by fpeaking loud,

And Holy words grow vile, uf'd by the Croud.

As long ago when fpeaking loud was uf'd,

Some Shepherds learn't the words, and them abuf'd.

They put the Bread upon a Stone, then faid

The words, and ftraight Flefh of the Bread was made:

But fee to what amounts the Shepherds gains,

For Heav'n with Fire Confum'd them for their Pains.

Next private Maffes, where the Prieft alone *(m)*

Communicats, may Lawfully be done.

Of Sport alone, no doubt, wee've often heard,

But that this is a Contradiction's fear'd.

What CHRIST's command more Contradicts, D'ye think ?

Who

(k) Miffal Rom. in canon. miff. profert verba Confecrationis diftincte fecrete & attente. (l) Durand Ration. l. 4. de Secreta. (m) Bell de miff. l. 2. c. 9.

Who said to's Disciples, take, eat, and Drink?
Than for a Rav'nous Priest to gulp all down,
And bid the People Feed with looking on.
They teach, that CHRIST's intire in either kind,
The Cup's not for the Laity design'd : (*n*)
And seeing one is all as well as both,
To trouble Lay-men with the Cup they're loth.
But yet the Clergy, it should seem, do mind him,
Who far'd so ill for leaving's Drink behind him :
And therefore you, their Worships wise, may trust
Will not snap short, as the Blind Laicks must.
They teach, that CHRIST is truely really in (*o*)
The *Eucharist*, that is the Bread and Wine.
His Flesh, Blood, Bones, Divinity and Soul
There by a knack are all intire and whole.
Whole CHRIST must in a narrow compass be,
The Wafer's bulk is very small we see ;
Yet Oh bad luck, this Body you can neither
Perceive with Spectacles, nor touch it either
Nor doth it fill a place, as Bodies do,
And must; but hold a little, you shall know
This one and self same *Bodie* may be in,
A Hundred Thousand sev'ral places seen
At once, for it is Rat'nal to suppose,
The *Euch'rist* 's giv'n at once, in places more than those.

Our

(*n*) *Concil. Trid. Seff. 21. c. 2. 3.* (*o*) *Conc. Trid. Seff. 13. c. 1. Bell de Euch. l. 1. c. 2.*

Our SAVIOUR faid to *Thomas*, feel and fee,
But better Skill'd in Logicks pop'lings be.
The Bread is chang'd, they teach 'tis Bread no more, *(p)*
But JESUS's Body which we fhould adore.
The Wine, or rather Wine and Water mix'd
Hey *Prefto's* gone, and Blood in place o't fix'd.
See how your Senfes thus the Priefts beguile,
Of Bread and Wine here's Figure, form, and fmell,
And taft, yet not one bit or drop the while.
A true Believer in this Popifh plot
Who'd be, muft firft commence an Errant Sot:
His fenfe as well as Reafon loft, they both muft be forgot.
For nothing's left, according to their Feigning,
But the Poor accidents alone remaining.
And fo thofe accidents believ't who lift,
Without a *Subject* muft (tis true) Subfift.
Here's Whitenefs, Roundnefs, Thinnefs as 'tis thought,
'Tis Whitenefs, Roundnefs, Thinnefs tho of nought.
CHRIST's Body is not (they confefs) white, round,
And thin; and Bread here is not to be found.
If CHRIST his Body ate, and drank his Blood,
Why, then I think we fairly may conclude
His Blood and Body at the Table was,
Yet did through his own Mouth and Stomach pafs.
'Twas broke, yet whole, eat, yet uneaten, nay

(p) *Conc. Trid. Sefs.* 13. *c.* 4. & *Can.* 2. &c.

His Blood was Shed, and in the Cup they say,
He Drank't himself, yet not one Drop'tis plain
Was missing all this while from any Vein.
The eater was the eaten thing, and the
Thing eaten, was the eater too we see.
Those who Delight to Learn in *Bedlam* Schools,
May hear the Ravings of such Sp'ritual Fools.
Each Sorry Priest this feat too can perform,
Who as he should do, doth pronounce that Charm
Of theirs (for such they make it) *hoc est enim*
(I think the other words are) *corpus meum.*
And so a Wretched Mortal Sinful elf,
Doth more than e'er th' Almighty did himself
He by his word from nothing Creatures Rear'd,
And their Orig'nal nothing disappear'd ;
But these Blasphemers by their words command
A Creature to Commence a GOD, and for their maker stand.
Not only one such Deity they make,
Thousands of Thousands in a Day they Bake,
Their GODS are plentifull as Wafer Cake.
And the *Bran Idol* to a Deity (*q*)
Thus Charm'd, must be fall'n down to and Ador'd,
And Worship't as the Sacred Majesty,
Of Heav'n and Earth, ev'n JESUS CHRIST our LORD.
All ye most Sottish 'mong the Heathen come,

And

(*q*) *Concil. Trid. Seff.* 13. *c.* 5. *& Can.* 6.

And learn Idolatry from Chriſtian *Rome*.
Thou Heathen *Rome* of wiſe Men did'ſt Delight
To make your GODS, or of the bold in Fight.
The *Greeks*, e'er *Rome* was built for your aboad,
A Rat'nal Creature choſe to be their GOD.
Th' *Ægyptians* ſtill more brutiſh than the reſt,
Had yet for their chief GOD (*r*) a living beaſt.
But ſee, the *Pope* for his chief GOD doth take
A ſenſeleſs lifeleſs thing, a Wafer Cake :
Firſt Sow'n, then mow'd, then brought into the Barn,
Theie Threſht, then in the Mill they grind the Corn:
Sifted and kneaded, back'd and then at laſt,
The Toaſted Cake is Godded by the Prieſt.
Becauſe this is not vile enough as yet, (*s*)
They Sacrifice this GOD of theirs, unto
Their GOD, what tho no Blood from it they get,
As *Jews* and Heathens from their victims do ?
A Sacrifice 'tis ne'er the leſs, and weie
CHRIST in their reach, we reaſon have to fear, ⎫
They'd make him Bleed of new, and with his Members fare. ⎭
An Jcy horror chills my Freezing Blood,
I Scarce dare name the mighty Draughts, they've drunk of this
But all their wicked follys to compleat,   'ſame Flood
At laſt the Savage makes the GOD his Meat.
On Humane Fleſh the *Carribbeans* fed,

G   But

<hr>

(*r*) *Apis*. (*s*) *Concil. Tiid. Seſſ.* 22. c. 12. &c.

But, that they're Saints to Papifts, may be faid :
Vile Wretches they, no Truth's in their aboad,
Who Barb'roufly Devour their very GOD.
Well fare the Prince of Orators, who faid, *(t)*
Was any Mortal ever yet fo mad,
As to believe the thing he eateth is
His GOD. The *Pope* he knew not, I confefs ;
But yet he very kindly did prepare
The Name of Mad-man, for his Hol'nefs fhare.
Their Fulfom *Euch'rift* what can Parallel,
What Engine hath the Magazine of Hell
More apt than this, for beating down at once
Religion, reafon, yea and common Sence ?
Their Sacraments to Senfe have no pretence,
Of Folly they're the very quinteffence,
Of hated falfehood, grofs abfurdity,
Blafphemy, and profane Idolatry.
Who e'er denys this Truth, muft be a fool,
With Brazen forehead and a leaden Skull.
Heav'n hates, the Earth fhould furely them abhore,
They're only fit for Hell, from whence they came before.
From what is faid, I think it does appear,
Than Days bright Lamp, which fhines at noon, more clear,
The Pop'lings may be empty Clouds defign'd, *(u)*
Who're whirl'd about by ev'ry giddy Wind.

Im-

(t) *Cicero de nat. deor. l.* 3. *Ecquem tam amentem effe putas, qui illud quo vef-catur deum credat effe?* (u) *Jude,* v. 12.

Impiety *and* Superstition

EXPOS'D,

A Poetical ESSAY.

PART. II.

Jude, part of the 4*th* Verse.

Ungodly Men turning the Grace of our GOD *into Lasciviousness.*

THE *Consulean* Orator, of Old, (*a*)
    The Common-wealth's approaching fate foretold.
    For why ? the Names of things were lost away,
It needs must Sink and feel a quick Decay.
When vice is by the name of virtue Grac'd,
And virtue by a vitious name Debaf'd ;
Then who's so Blind ? That sees not danger near,

Who

_____

(*a*) *Orat:* contra Catalin.

Who does not in the Church some mighty changes fear?
Whil'st Drunk'ness we excuse, or Mitigate,
And Drunkards, by the Name of heartie greet
Vile Avarice, we Parsimony name,
And Prodigals, the name of Lib'ial claim.
And he who on his back wears an Estate,
Is Fashionable nam'd, Genteel or Neat.
But Oh! what's most pestiferous of all,
A certain token of the Churches fall.
The Liberty by CHRIST acquir'd 's abus'd,
And for a cloak to Sin by wicked men is us'd.
Our GOD did grant us a secure retreat, (b)
Where we might shun the Furries Scroching heat,
He from the Pow'r of Darkness us set free,
That in his Darling's Kingdom we might be.
How can we then think wee're Translated from,
Vile Lusts, that still in viler we may roam?

But few there be 'tis true, who frankly will
Themselves acknowledge Guilty of this ill;
Yet Search their Lives, and straight we must Confess,
Ev'n the Reform'd Stain'd with Ungodliness,
Who turn Gods Grace into Lasciviousness.

'Tis of GODS Grace, some to Salvation be
Predestinate from all Eternitie.

Yet

(b) Colog. c. 1. v. 13.

Yet Wicked men there are, who turn this Grace
Of our Good God, into Lasciviousness.
And thus they Argue, I'me Elected, then
How e'er I live I shall be sav'd. Again,
I'me not Elect, then I shall Damned be,
Tho all I can, or will,'s perform'd by me :
I can't be sav'd. In pleasures let me range,
For the Almighty's Counsel cannot change.
These hated Libertins vile Lives declare
Them not Reform'd, no sure deform'd they are,
And tho amongst the Protestants they lurch,
They're not the genuine of-spring of the Church.
For as the end it self is fore-ordain'd,
So are the Mediums that to it tend.
And who's predestin'd to Eternal Light,
Faith and Good works will surely never Slight.
E'er this great Fabrick of the World was made, (c)
E'er the Foundations of the Earth were laid,
In CHRIST (Our God) Elected us, that we
Holy and blameless in his sight should be.
Then he who makes not Holy Life his care,
Can not among the Elect claim a share.
What Soldier's such a Fool to think his pay
Is due, tho he refuses to obey.
Ev'n Nature tells us, those should be belov'd

_____

(c) *Ephes.* c. I. v. 4.

By us, whofe tendernefs we firft have prov'd.
When once our Hearts have felt the divine Fire,
We then fhall Burn with mutual defire.
We Love the LORD, the mighty GOD above, (d)
Becaufe he firft beftow'd on us his Love.
In this confifts our Love to GOD, that we (e)
Should of his Precepts ftrict Obfervers be.
And this his Precept is, that we believe (f)
On his Son JESUS's name, that we may Live:
And that we all fhould one another Love,
In doing this our Love to GOD we prove.
So *John* from this (that we are now the Sons (g)
Of GOD, and yet it don't appear what we
Shall be, but this we furely know when once
He fhall appear, that like him we fhall be
For as he is, wee'll fee him) doth conclude,
The Man that hath this hope will needs be Good
To Purifie himfelf he will be fure,
For why he know'th his Heav'nly Father's pure.
Peter the Brethren bids great care to take, (h)
That they may fure their own Election make.
By what? ev'n by good Works, for why he had
A Catalogue of thefe before them laid.
For whom he did Predeftinate; them he (i)
Did alfo call, and call'd did juftify.

Y

(d) 1. *John* c. 4. v: 19. (e) *John* c. 14. v: 23. (f) 1. *John* c. 3. v: 23. (g) 1. *John* c. 3. v: 2. & 3. (h) 2. *Peter* c. 1. v: 10. (i) *Rom.* c. 8. v: 30.

I am the Vine, fays CHRIST our LORD, and ye (k)
The Branches are, he that abides in me,
And I in him, he fpreads his Loaden Boughs,
From whofe rare fruit a pleafing Liquor flows.

Others there be, who God's long fuff'ring Grace,
And Mercy turn into Lafcivioufnefs.
Say they, Heav'ns boundlefs Mercies all men know,
To pardon eafy, and to punifh flow.
And tho our weighty Sins for Judgement cry,
Yet ftill he doth the threatned pains delay.
Befides, the Wickcd in this World below
Do molt in Riches, and in Honours flow :
Then why fhould I Repent ? no I'll delay,
And taft the fweets of Youth while yet I may :
The Gates of Heav'n and Grace, will fure unlock,
When ever I find leafure time to knock.
Thus Boys the Malter flight, when they perceive
Him too indulgent, eafy to forgive.
Paul heav'ly taxes wicked Men who choofe (l)
GOD's Mercy and forbearance to abufe.
The Riches of his Goodnefs, do'ft defpife,
Forbearance and Long-fuffering, he crys:
Not knowing that the goodnefs of thy GOD,
Of Penitence, points out to thee the road.
But for the hardnefs of thy Heart, which knows

Not

Not to repent, thou wickedly haſt choſe
By adding ſtill freſh Sins unto thy ſcore,
Againſt the day of wrath, wrath to thy ſelf to ſtore.
For tho' GOD's Mercy doth no limits know,
His Juſtice muſt have ſatisfaction too :
Theſe Attributes in equal ballance lye,
And neither muſt the others Right deny.
According to thy Deeds eternal bleſs,
Will be thy lot, or endleſs Miſeries.
Forgivneſs is with thee (ſays David) why ? (m)
That wee ſhould heap contempt, and blaſphemy.
No (never ſuch a Reaſon yet was heard)
But thou forgiveſt, that thou may'ſt be feard.
Beware thou ſay, I've long, unpuniſh'd, ſinn'd,
Leſt Heav'n this for an Anſwer to thee ſend ; (n)
Theſe things thou did'ſt, becauſe I ſilent was,
'Till thou thought'ſt wickedly, that I might paſs
For ſuch as thou, but I'll reprove thy ways,
And ſet thy Sins in rank before thine eyes.
Repent in time, for this ye know, that how (o)
When Eſau would the wiſh'd-for bleſs purſue,
He was reject, no penitence he found ;
Altho his manly cheeks in bring tears were drown'd.
How know'ſt thou that thy days will longer laſt?
Or can'ſt thou yet repent when thoſe are paſt ?

Why

(m) Pſal. 130. v. 4. (n) Pſal. 50. v. 21. (o) Hebrews 12. v. 17.

Why do'ft thou thus thy penitence delay ?
What if Heav'n fhould cut fhort thy long wifh'd day ?
God for thy long contempt may juftly fend
Judicial hardnefs, on thy dark'ned mind.
And when the Flouds come rolling from thine eyes,
Ev'n then he may thy Tears and Pray'rs defpife.
For who in Health his Threat'nings flight, 'tis fear'd,
When Death alarms them, they fhall not be heard.
So fays the Lord, becaufe ye made your choice (p)
Still to refufe my yet inviting Voice.
I Reach'd my hand to help you on your way,
Yet none regarded, no man did obey ,
But all my Counfel ye have fet at nought,
Nor my Reproofs ye would, nor yet them fought ,
I'll likewife laugh at your Calamity,
And I will mock you, when your fears draw nigh
When the Dread ftroak fhall come, which you fo fear,
And fwift as Defolation fhall appear,
Rolling like furly billows, when they rife
And Foaming mad, attack the Lowring Skies.
When like th' unwifh'd, unlook'd for whirlwind, your
Deftruction fhall your troubled minds o'er pow'r,
When fad Diftrefs and heavie Anguifh, fhall
Rufhing on you, Deject both great and fmall ;
Then, not till then, they'll call on me, but I

H

Will

_____

(p) *Prov.* c. 1. v: 24. 25. 26. 27. 28.

Will not them hear, nor Anſwer when they cry. (q)
They'll ſeek me, e'er the riſing morn diſplay
The Purple Enſigns of approaching day :
But me they ſhall not find, for Wiſdom's Voice
They Loath'd, and to fear Heav'n was not their choice.

Who Gods long ſuff'ring Grace have felt, yet ſtill
Put of Repentance for a diſtant while.
Are like the ſturdy Thievs, who ſay go to,
Let's Rob and Plunder as we us'd to do :
Why ſhould we fear? the Judge has ſtill been kind,
Nor need we doubt, but ſtill he'll be our Friend.
'Tho Mercy boundleſs be ; yet we ſhould know
That Juſtice muſt have Satisfaction too.

Nor ſhould we, tho ſome wicked men grow great,
Or Imitate their Crimes, or yet envy their State,
For they ſhall be cut down like tender Graſs, (r)
Or like the Blooming Flow'r which ſoon doth paſs.
So have I ſeen a villain trade the Stage,
Intirely Govern'd by his luſt and rage,
Succesfull he, his nod the Croud obey,
But the fifth Act took all his Pow'r away :
His Broider'd Robes were Roll'd in Purple gore,
His by-paſt Happineſs ; but made his Anguiſh more.

Our

(q) Prov. c. 1. v: 28 & 29. (r) Pſal. 37. v: 2.

Our SAVIOUR CHRIST from Bondage fet us free,
He us Redeem'd from our Iniquitie.
Yet fome there be, who turn this matchlefs Grace
Of our Blefs'd LORD into Lafcivioufnefs.
Who think the Liberty acquir'd by CHRIST,
Licenfes them to Act what Sins they lift.
And thus thefe brutal Men themfelves exprefs,
Had we not Sinn'd, Heav'ns Glory had been lefs.
GOD Pardons Sin, which gains him moft applaufe,
So Good effects proceed from an ill caufe.
In *Paul* th' Apoftles time, of fuch, were fome, (s)
Who fay'd, let us do ill, that Good may come.
Sin heap on Sin, for ftill the more wee're found (t)
In Sin, the Grace of GOD will more abound.
Th' Apoftle Anfwers GOD forbid, fhall we (u)
Who're Dead to Sin, live in Iniquitie.
Nor did that ftream come from our SAVIOUR's fide,
That we fhould in our fordid Lufts abide :
That healing torrent was on purpofe fpilt,
To wafh our Stains, and Expiate our Guilt.
Then fure we fhould Ungodlinefs abhore, (x)
Deny the Worldly lufts, we Lov'd before ;
Sobriety fhould be our future care,
And Holy Lives, whilft in this World we are.

Some,

(s) *Rom. c.* 3. v. 8. (t) *Rom. c.* 6. v. 1.   (u) *Rom. c.* 6. v. 2   (x) *Titus c.* 2.
v: 12.

Some, fince the *Jewifh-Sabbath's* ta'en away,
Think they need not obferve a feventh day.
(Hence fprung the Book of fports, hence, *(y) Heylins* Book,
And hence our, *(z)* Modern Mad-cap, his oppinions took.)
Thefe think, the LORD fix days for work appoints,
A feventh too, to Exercife their Joints.
Shooting at butts, or Dancing of the Hay,
No doubt are pleafant ways to Sanctifie the day.
The Prim'tive Chrift'ans on the firft day met, *(a)*
Broke Bread, and heard the word, nor did forget *(b)*
To call on GOD, and deal their Charity;
But not on word of fporting by the by.
Had our high flyers been *Difciples* then,
Eutychus might with Dancing got a ftrain,
Which foon might cure, but would not as we Read,
Or got fo great a fall, or been ta'en up quite Dead.

Under pretext of Chrift'an liberty,
Some their deprav'd defires indulge we fee.
Prone to Lafcivioufnefs, they're fet on Fire
By Youth, and flaves to ev'ry vain defire.
Dancing upon the head of thefe appears,
And as it does deferve the Garland wears.
Comus thou waft the GOD of Roaring Boys,
Who fill'd the Midnight Streets with Songs and Noife:

Drunk-

(y) *Hift. Sabbath.* (z) *Rehearfal.* (a) *Acts* c. 20. v: 7. &c. (b) 1. *Corinth.*
c. 16. v: 2.

Drunkards and Wantons were thy guard du corps,
Who did with dance, and fidle thee adore;
From houſe to houſe they 'bout the City reel,
No door ſo ſtrong, but did their courage feel.
Windows and Sign-poſts too in pieces fly,
And all about the ſtreets the Shivers ly.
Well pleaſ'd with Miſchiefs done, there reſts one more
Undone, to call the ſleeping Nimph a Whore:
Fidles ſtrike up, hey for a light, and then
The Doughty *Heroes* march to Bed again.
Beſotted Man, leave leaping to the ſtag, *(c)*
Who skips from hill to hill, from craig to craig. *(d)*
Skipping and leaping well becomes the Rams, *(e)*
A quality inherent too in Lambs,
And Calves come skipping from their lowing dams.
So Satyrs, in their groves conſulted skip, *(f)*
And future things declare, by handſom trip.
Ye fair ones know, nor dancing, nor good cheer,
Is gladeneſs, but to keep ones conſcience clear.
Your Virgin modeſty muſt needs give place,
Where dancing well is thought a charming Grace.
Ev'n more than fury, dancing hurted hath,
A Dancer's *Præmium* was a *(g)* Prophet's Death.
The Daughter of a Queen, bred in loves School,
Before the Men is brought, to play the fool:

What

(c) *Iſa.* 35. v. 6. (d) *Cantich.* 2. v. 8. (e) *Pſal.* 114. v. 4. (f) *Iſa.* 13. v. 21. (g) *John Baptiſt.*

What elfe from an Adult'refs could fhe learn,
But pawn her modefty her Bread to earn.
See when our Dancers meet, or at a Ball.
In pubick School, or in fome private hall.
See how the Snow-white Breaft's expos'd to view,
Which heaving prefs the bafhful youth to wooe.
Sure there's infection in their very breath,
Their beautious Eyes dart unavoided Death.
Would you be bleft? ev'n Daphnefs eyes contemn,
Tho' other fair-ones eyes feem borrow'd Lights to them.
Roufe then, ye Parents of the Northern Climes,
Learn fiom the Scriptures to prevent fuch Crimes.
Let the Adult'refs Daughter dance, but let
The Chaft, the Modeft, true Religion get.

Heaven's common Gifts fome wickedly abufe,
While other Sots are wantonly profufe.
Our Hearts are fill'd with gladnefs ev'ry field
Unhop'd, unwifh'd for, plenteous Crops doth yield;
Yet an Ungodly Mercenary crew,
Grudge at the Blefs, O may they be but few,
Who fuch a Dev'lifh Character deferve,
To cram their private chefts, would fee a Nation ftarve.
While others fottifhly do ufe the blefs,
As if't were giv'n to feed Lafcivioufnefs.
Soon as the Barn and rav'nous Bellie's ftor'd, (b)

The

(b) *Hofea* 13. v. 6.

The Heart's lift up, and they forget the LORD.

Heav'n with uncommon Wisdom some endues,
Yet mark how basely some this Gift abuse,
To work their Neighbours hurt; such to do ill (*i*)
Are wise, but to do good, they have no skill.
The *Isra'lites* said *Phar'oh*, num'rous grow, (*k*)
And might'er than th' *Ægyptians*, come let's show
Our prudent care, against this People, lest
They grow so strong, wee sha'n't get them suppreft.
While some to wickedness so bend their wit, (*l*)
They cannot sleep unless some mischief hit.
Unless by them some innocent's oppreft,
Th' abortive mischief keeps their eyes from rest.
For Wickedness as daily bread they use,
And vi'lence is the luscious Wine they choose,
Amnon thus with incestuous lust possest, (*m*)
The ill undone, his eyes could find no rest.
Some others bent, the Church, are to destroy,
Or its pure Worship mix, with base alloy.
The Princes of the Earth their Counsels twist, (*n*)
Against *Jehovah*, and against his CHRIST.
Rome, with such Consultations doth abound,
The Gospel Purity, for to confound.
Fools they, who's wife? ev'n he that fears the LORD, (*o*)

Who

(*i*) *Jerem.* 4 v. 22. (*k*) *Exod.* 1. v. 9, & 10. (*l*) *Prov.* 4. v. 16. & 17.
(*m*) 2 *Sam.* 13. v. 2. (*n*) *Psal.* 2. v. 2. (*o*) *Job* 28. v. 28.

Who underftands ? But he by whom ill is abhor'd.

Health is the Gift of Heav'n, a Clown in health,
Excels the Churl infirm, who fweems in wealth.
Yet, fome in gluttony cut fhort their day,
Or in deep Draughts, do fwill their health's away.
Self-Murd'rers they, for who hath forrow, who (p)
Hath woe, 'mong whom do due contentions flow.
Who Babbles, who without a caufe hath Wounds,
Or whofe fcorch'd eye with rednefs fo abounds.
Ev'n his who ftill does ply the fparkling wine,
That poif'nous Juice of the pernicious vine.
For treach'rous Wine does fatal Weapons bear,
The glafs is more deftructive than the Spear.
Drunkards with Idols may be well compar'd,
For tho' they've Ears, no found by them is heard.
Their Nofes fmell not, neither does the Light
Chear with kind infl'ence, their now ufelefs fight.
Tho' Mouths they want not, they're unfkill'd to talk.
Tho Hands and Feet they have, they neither feel nor walk.

And as intemp'rance burfts the glutted veins,
So when the Tyrant Luft, i'th' body reigns,
Th' Invenom'd Blood with vi'lent fury burns,
And to a Thoufand diff'rent Tortures turns.

It

It roots the fear of Heav'n out of the mind,
Sage *Solomon's* an inftance of this kind.
Thus the fond Elders by their fight mifled,
Purfu'd the Joys of a forbidden bed,
Nor could the luftfull Flame be difpoffeft,
Till with a fhow'r of Weighty ftones Suppreft.
By it the Strongeft men are Proftrate laid,
Thus *Samfon* by his *Dalilah* betray'd,
Was hers, and then his En'mies captive made.
To poverty it leads with eagre haft,
It made the Prodigal his Portion waft,
Till Starv'd by Riot, and with want oppreft,
He fed with Swine, himfelf the greater beaft.
To thofe who Simples Sov'rein virtue know,
And to their ends, can well apply them too :
Thofe who their Skill in Tedious confults try,
How to give eafe to Humane Mifery,
I leave to Sing, how luft doth fo exhale,
And quite dry up the moifture Radicale :
How't kills the Nat'ral heat, and does arreft
Digeft'on, hence the Stomach is oppreft
With Crudities, hence Corrupt Blood doth flow,
And hence the fainting limbs a burthen grow.
The Drooping head fly's to the hands for aid,
But by the feeble props is foon betray'd.

I

Then

Then fhun a Whore, ev'n in thy youthfull days, (q)
Let not thy heart decline into her ways.
Let not her lureing eyes thy mind entice,
Nor let her fmiles delude thy dazled eyes.
Let not her pratle, thy fond Soul betray,
Let not her paths diftract thee from the way,
Who follow's her undoubtedly muft ftray.
For fhe the Fool into her fnare decoys,
And by pretended Happinefs deftroys.
How many Wounded men hath fhe caft down ?
And thofe who for their Sing'lar ftrength were known,
By' her have been cut of, her dwellings lead
To Hell; and to the Chambers of the Dead.
Above the nets they thought a leap to take,
But Headlong dropt into th' Infernal lake.

Beautie that fignal gift, that greateft blifs,
Too many turn into Lafcivioufnefs.
A lure they make it, to draw others in,
And force th' unfixed wand'ring mind to Sin.
Nor pleaf'd with Beautie nature doth beftow,
They Rectify't by all the Arts they know,
With Spanifh Wool red as the Blooming Rofe,
And cerufe whiter than the Mountain Snows:
With patches Marfhall'd on the Face with Art,

And

And all to catch a *Ninny*'s wand'ring heart.
How fluctuating's Beautie, O how vain,
Which ev'ry flight difeafe doth taint and ftain.
When GOD corrects for Sin, the Beauties fade, (r
Man looks like Cloath by fretting moths decay'd.
Favour's deceitfull, fadeing Beautie's vain, (s)
But fhe that fears the LORD, fhall lafting Praifes gain.
And by experience taught, we know the fair
May with the Sodom apples well compare :
Which charm the eye, the outfide only feen,
But Worms and Rottennefs are Lodg'd within.
Then let no fuch vain toy's affect your mind,
Which meet with no Admirers but the Blind.
Love you the LORD ? No borrow'd Beauties prize,
No Artificial charms attract his eyes.
Th' Almighty only rates a fpotelefs heart,
And for its fake accepts each other part.

'Tis he beftows on men their ftrength and Pow'r, (t)
Yet moft abufe thefe gifts t'opprefs the Poor. (u)
The bulky Champion of *Philiftias* hoft,
His Iron nerves, his finews brafs did boaft :
Puft up, his ftrength againft the LORD he'd try,
And th' Armies of the Living GOD defie,
And yet a ftripling raif'd by Heav'n, made him extended ly.

(r) *Pfal.* 39. v: 11. (s) *Prov. c.* 31. v: 30. (t) *Pfal.* 68. v: 35. (u) *James* 2.
v. 6.

For who abuſe their ſtrength, or Pow'r, may know,
GOD never lets th'abuſe unpuniſh'd go.
Moſes and *Aaron* to th' *Ægyptian* told, (x)
The LORD requir'd the *Iſraelites* to hold
A Feaſt to him, and bad him let them go,
Yet ſtill the *Tyrant Phar'oh* anſwer'd no.
Who is the LORD? That I ſhould him obey,
To let them go, I know him not, not I,
Nor will I let them go, thus did he GOD defie.
But tho he would not know *Jehova* now,
Yet to his hurt, he afterwards him knew,
Nor did *Sennacherib* unpuniſh'd go,
His Blaſphemy procur'd his overthrow:
His Mighty hoſt was by an Angel ſlain,
And with Paternal Blood, his Sons, themſelves did ſtain.

That Wealth's the gift of Heav'n, we can't deny, (y)
Unleſs we give ſage *Solomon* the lye.
Yet Oh, how few aright the Bliſs do uſe,
How many diff'rent ways do men this gift abuſe?
Gain to their thoughts, ſuch ſweets does repreſent,
That how to gain, is all their minds intent.
Their Precious time in its purſuit they ſpend,
As if Salvation did on it depend.
Yea Gold does ſo mens Noble Souls debaſe,

f That

(x) *Exod. c. 5. v. 1. & 2.* (y) *Prov. c. 10. v. 22.*

That they their Heav'n in such a triffle place.
Strange thirst of Wealth ! they place their hope in Gold, (z)
And put their confidence in rip'ned Mold.
Unthinking Men, they Earth to Heav'n prefer,
And fading Joys, to endless Glory there.

Nor doth the Miser reach at Happiness,
His Wealth possesses him, he does not it possess.
He's not the Master of his hoarded Trash,
No, he's a Servant, yea a slave to Cash.
He's still oppress'd with fear, and Misery,
Ev'n Children may be wiser thought than he ;
For they from Counters, currant Money know,
Almost as soon as they have learn't to go ;
But he esteemeth counterfeit Delights,
Before the Joys to which kind Heav'n invites.
And where's his gain ? tho' over-charg'd with Gold ?
His bursting Coffers can't their Burthen hold.
For this can ne'er his troubled mind appease
Nor buy his Sorrows ev'n a minutes ease.

Some on their Bellies all their Wealth bestow,
That fill'd, they wish no other Bless to know.
Let's Eat and Drink, these Epicur'ans cry,
While 'tis to day, to morrow we must dye.

Drop

_____

(z) *Job.* 31. v. 24.

Dives, for such a wretch, stands on record,
Whose only Bless was a well furnish'd Board.
And such snuff at the Meat, their Palat's nice,
Unless some *Monsieur* poison it with spice.
'Gainst Heav'n they sin, who thus with eagre haste
On Feasting do their Patrimony waste.
They're but Trustees, then Oh! how shall their Fears
Encrease, when this Allarm shall reach their Ears?
How you have manadg'd, Mortal, let me see?
For thou no longer must a Steward be.
And with themselves they seem a War to wage,
Who waste in Youth, the supports of old Age;
For he who does the sparkling Liquor ply, (a)
And of his Mighty Strength in Drinking brags,
Shall with the Glutton come to Poverty,
And Drowsiness shall cloath a Man with Rags.
Against his Children too he sins, for he
In Riot wastes what should their comfort be.
Nor Beast, nor Bird, with him wee can compare,
They pinch themselves, to make their young ones better fare.
They rob the truely poor ones of their Bread,
Who quaff deep draughts of Wine in mighty bowls,
And with *Assyrian* Ointments 'noint the Head,
Yet *Joseph's* Sorrow does not reach their Souls

Again

Again,

Riches in fome fo ftrikes the Judgement blind,
That Pride's falfe light m fguides the wand'ring mind.
Hence Luxury ir cloaths hath grown fo great,
And is the a our Britifh State:
It's ghty cry hath reach'd th' Almighty's Throne,
And calls, my teat's a weighty vengeance down :
Which had no doubt e'er now on us been pour'd,
Had not the Godly's Pray'rs a Sift procur'd.
For th' Apoftolick truth ftill firm hath ftood,
That the Almighty doth refift the Proud. (c)
Thus God of old, the Luxury reveng'd
Of _Sions_ Daughters, and to grief it chang'd.
So fay'th the LORD,
Since _Sions_ Daughters are fo haughty grown, (d)
With ftretcht forth Necks, they flide along the Town.
With wanton Eyes they lure whom e'er they meet,
And mincing, make a tinkling with their feet.
Therefore
No more they fhall a towring head drefs need,
For with a Scab _(fays_ GOD_)_ I'll fmite the head.
No more embroid'red rayments they fhall fhew,
For ev'n what nature hides, fhall be expos'd to view.
All their fine tinkling Ornaments that day,

Cauls

(c) I _Peter_ 5. v. 5. (d) _Ijaiah_ 3. v. 16, 17, & 18.

Cauls, and round tires, the LORD will take away. *(e)*
Their Rubbie Chains that round their Necks they wear,
And Golden Bracelets which their Arms do bear,
Mufflers and Bonnets that adorn the Head,
And Ornaments which o'er their Legs are spread:
Head-bands and Tablets now no more appear,
Nor double Pearls to hang the loaded Ear.
No Diamond Ring the Finger shall adorn,
Nor shall Nose Jewels any more be worn.
No more shall they be cloath'd with gay attire,
Who changing colours now so much admire,
No Mantles, Wimples, no, nor Crispin Pin,
Nor Looking-glass, shall be hereafter seen.
Ægyptian Linnen now their Pride to wear,
And Hoods, and costly Vails shall disappear.
In stead of Rich *Arabian* perfume,
A nauseous, loathed, stink shall fill the room.
A Rent shall be in thy rich Girdles stead :
To Curls and Locks which did adorn thy Head,
A hated scorned baldness shall succeed.
And for the Stomacher which now is wore,
(Sackcloth shall gird thee) thou shalt wear't no more.
Thy Beauty, which is now so much thy care,
The Sun shall burn, the thing so much you fear.
Thy Men slain by the Sword shall scatter'd ly,

Thy

(e) *Isaiah* 3. v. 18, 19, 20, 21, 22, 23, 24, & 25.

Thy mighty Men who durſt thy foes defy :
Thoſe who 'gainſt Fire and Sword, ſo boldly ſtood,
Shall fall in War, and under foot be trod.

Sure they to madneſs muſt be near aly'd,
Who in their Cloathing ſo themſelves do pride.
Our Cloaths are Witneſs of our perfidie,
And diſobedience to the Deitie :
Hence we our nakedneſs, and ſhame deriv'd,
And Skins of Beaſts to cover both receiv'd :
For this wee were from *Eden* juſtly driv'n,
The curſe of Earth, and the contempt of Heav'n.
Sure then,
While thus we daub with Gold and Silver Lace,
Wee render more conſpicuous our diſgrace.
Suppoſe a Robber were condemn'd to dye,
Yet pardon'd, on condition he ſhould ty
A Rope about his neck, and no pretence
ſhould thence remove't, till Death ſhould ſnatch him hence:
Now if his Rope with Gold and Silver he
Adorn, who would from madneſs think him free,
Who thus did pride himſelf in Infamy.

There's not a few, oh were their number leſs,
Who turn the Scriptures to Laſciviouſneſs,
And thereby authorize their Wickedneſs.

A free Gift is the sacred Writ, yea 'tis
The gift of Gifts, giv'n by the LORD of Bless.
Yet as the Fowler with his hidden snare,
Contrives t' intrap the Racers of the Air.
Their Voice he imitates, and so decoys
The simple Birds, he afterwards destroys.
Just so the Hereticks do make their choice,
To imitate our Blessed SAVIOUR's Voice,
Or his *Apostles*, that th' unwary they
May catch, and to perditions Gulph betray.
As Pirats, Ships, on hidden Rocks entice,
And by false Fires delude Sea-farers Eyes.
So Hereticks the Scriptures wrest, that Fools
May be entic'd, to wrack their precious Souls.

Some from the Scriptures seek Authority,
For ev'ry Mischief and Impiety.
So that of *Paul*, no longer Water drink,   (*f*)
But for thy Stomach, use a litle Wine,
And thine Infirmities : our Tiplers think,
Allows them to drink deep, as they incline.
But did they one Text more peruse, they'd find (*g*)
Heav'n never was for drunken sots design'd.

The cov'tous wretch, who puts his Trust in Gold,
Thinks on that Scripture Text he may lay hold ;

If

(*f*) 1 *Tim.* 5. v. 23. (*g*) 1 *Corinth.* 6. v. 10.

If any for his own doth not provide, (h)
For thofe who with him in his Houfe abide,
Worfe than an Infidel he is, the Faith he hath deny'd.
But mark the Charge that's given by *Paul*, to thofe (i)
Wh' abound in Worldly Wealth, on whom it flows.
Let not Prides flatuous humour fwell thy Veins,
Nor truft in Riches which away do fly;
But truft in GOD, who lives, and ever reigns,
And gives us richly all things to enjoy.

And our Non-jurant, unbelieving Priefts, (k)
The facred Scripture Text do thus abufe;
Who'd make a free-born People worfe than Beafts,
Meer Tools to ferve a *French* Knight-Errant's ufe.]
Fools, fee they not a plain diftinction here,
betwixt the Powers that are not, and that are.
A Pow'r may be pretended, where there's none,
James fign'd Commiffions, tho' the King was gone,
Ev'n after he had forfeited the Throne. (l)
And fuch, while here, was his difpenfing pow'r,
Which at one gulp did all our rights devour.
But mark, the higher pow'rs herein expreft,
Are pow'rs that be, that is, that do exift:

K 2

Thefe

(h) 1 *Tim.* 5. v. 8. (i) 1 *Tim.* 6. v. 17. (k) *Rom.* 13. v. 1, & 2.
*Let every Soul be fubject unto the higher Powers. for there is no Power but
of GOD. the Powers that be, are ordained of GOD.* v. 2. *Whofoever therefore refifteth the Power, refifteth the Ordinance of GOD, and they that refift,
fhall receive to themfelves Damnation.* (l) Claim of Right.

These are of God, and who resists these pow'rs,
A sure Damnation to himself procures.
Sure any but a bigot fool will grant,
Pow'rs that are not, who legal pow'r do want;
Are not the higher pow'rs herein exprest,
Nor shall Damnation sease them, who such pow'rs resist.
But mark, crys Tory, who the Scepter Sway'd,
'Twas Tyrant *Nero*, who must be obey'd.
I Answer thus, the People did consent:
Augustus brought into the Government
A Constitution new, and all were well content.
And now supposing *Nero* rul'd thereby,
None could resist him, nay they should obey.
For sure the pow'rs that be in any state,
Are by its Constitution regulate.
And so had *Nero* with the Law's dispenf'd,
He should for the Resister been Sentenc'd.
For who, Dispensing pow'r place in the Crown,
A pow'r Superior to the Law's do own.
A pow'r above the Law's, becomes their Death,
Dissolv'd by ev'ry blast of Kingly breath:
Thus loof'd, the Subject free as passing Air
May chufe what Government he pleafe to wear.
Now since the pow'rs that be, must be obey'd,
Not those that are not, as already said;

Then they who buftle for a Chevalier,
May, from this Text their own Damnation hear.

Now in fmooth running verfe, Harmonious Song,
My mufe fhall tell whence modern prophets fprung.
When Wind's pent up in Subterranean cave,
The Earth's convulfion'd 'till it freedom have :
Rack'd, fhe at length lays ope her gaping Womb,
To Men at once a Murth'rer and a Tomb.
   Ev'n fo,
Puft up with felf conceit, the fool mifcaries,
Who thinks, he's one of *Heavens* Secretaries.
For Prid's rank Poifon fwells th' exalted Mind,
Till he, a prophet thinks himfelf defign'd :
The Fabrick fhakes, the Prophet fweats and Nods,
As if he were poffeft by all the windy Gods.
The flatuous humour fo the Breaft doth heave,
No diffapointments can them undeceive.
This Poifon's of fo fubtile, ftrange a kind,
That the Believer's whirl'd about by the fame giddy Wind.

Since then, weak Men fo many ways abufe
GODS Grace, let us think on its end and ufe.
Then, Our great GOD Elected us that wee
May holy, and before him, blamelefs be, (*l.*)
And our few flying Minutes, pafs in Charitie.

Doth

Doth he forbear, hath he more Minutes lent ?
Then fure, thereby he leads us to Repent. (m)

Our SAVIOUR CHRIST Redeem'd us, bought us, why ?
But that we fhould th' Almighty glorify, (n)
As in our Bodies, in our Spirits too,
For they are GOD's, they from himfelf did flow.
Has he with fing'lar Graces us endued ?
Has he much Wifdom on our Minds beftow'd ?
Then this return, wee'll for his Goodnefs make,   (o)
Wee'll Praife his Name, and with glad Zeal the Cup of
                                        (Bleffing take

Bleft Author of my Life, O pity me,
Remove far from my Soul Impuritie.
And fince my Soul to Love will needs incline,
O my dear GOD, then let that Love be thine.
Grant in my Soul the World may have no part,
That fly Debaucher of my wand'ring heart.
In this low World no Medicine wee find,
Can eafe the reftlefs Torments of the Mind.
Thou, thou, O GOD alone, canft eafe our Grief,
With the pure Waters of the Well of Life.

Soc n

(m) Rom. 2. v. 4. (n) 1 Corinth. 6. v. 20. (o) Pfal. 116. v. 12, & 13.

Soon may that happy Day of Vision be,
When I shall make a near approach to thee :
When diftant Faith shall in near Vision cease,
And ftill my Love shall with my Sight increase.

F I N I S.

CPSIA information can be obtained at www.ICGtesting.com
Printed in the USA
BVOW01s1030240914

368160BV00020B/807/P